THE SUTRA OF QUEEN ŚRĪMĀLĀ
OF THE LION'S ROAR

THE VIMALAKĪRTI SUTRA

BDK English Tripiṭaka 20-I, 26-I

THE SUTRA OF QUEEN ŚRĪMĀLĀ OF THE LION'S ROAR

Translated from the Chinese
(Taishō Volume 12, Number 353)

by

Diana Y. Paul

THE VIMALAKĪRTI SUTRA

Translated from the Chinese
(Taishō Volume 14, Number 475)

by

John R. McRae

**Numata Center
for Buddhist Translation and Research**
2004

First Printing, 2004
ISBN: 1-886439-31-1
Library of Congress Catalog Card Number: 2004113588

Published by
Numata Center for Buddhist Translation and Research
2620 Warring Street
Berkeley, California 94704

Printed in the United States of America

A Message on the Publication of the English Tripiṭaka

The Buddhist canon is said to contain eighty-four thousand different teachings. I believe that this is because the Buddha's basic approach was to prescribe a different treatment for every spiritual ailment, much as a doctor prescribes a different medicine for every medical ailment. Thus his teachings were always appropriate for the particular suffering individual and for the time at which the teaching was given, and over the ages not one of his prescriptions has failed to relieve the suffering to which it was addressed.

Ever since the Buddha's Great Demise over twenty-five hundred years ago, his message of wisdom and compassion has spread throughout the world. Yet no one has ever attempted to translate the entire Buddhist canon into English throughout the history of Japan. It is my greatest wish to see this done and to make the translations available to the many English-speaking people who have never had the opportunity to learn about the Buddha's teachings.

Of course, it would be impossible to translate all of the Buddha's eighty-four thousand teachings in a few years. I have, therefore, had one hundred thirty-nine of the scriptural texts in the prodigious Taishō edition of the Chinese Buddhist canon selected for inclusion in the First Series of this translation project.

It is in the nature of this undertaking that the results are bound to be criticized. Nonetheless, I am convinced that unless someone takes it upon himself or herself to initiate this project, it will never be done. At the same time, I hope that an improved, revised edition will appear in the future.

It is most gratifying that, thanks to the efforts of more than a hundred Buddhist scholars from the East and the West, this monumental project has finally gotten off the ground. May the rays of the Wisdom of the Compassionate One reach each and every person in the world.

NUMATA Yehan
Founder of the English
Tripiṭaka Project

August 7, 1991

Editorial Foreword

In January 1982, Dr. NUMATA Yehan, the founder of the Bukkyō Dendō Kyōkai (Society for the Promotion of Buddhism), decided to begin the monumental task of translating the complete Taishō edition of the Chinese Tripiṭaka (Buddhist canon) into the English language. Under his leadership, a special preparatory committee was organized in April 1982. By July of the same year, the Translation Committee of the English Tripiṭaka was officially convened.

The initial Committee consisted of the following members: (late) HANAYAMA Shōyū (Chairperson), (late) BANDŌ Shōjun, ISHIGAMI Zennō, (late) KAMATA Shigeo, KANAOKA Shūyū, MAYEDA Sengaku, NARA Yasuaki, (late) SAYEKI Shinkō, (late) SHIOIRI Ryōtatsu, TAMARU Noriyoshi, (late) TAMURA Kwansei, URYŪZU Ryūshin, and YUYAMA Akira. Assistant members of the Committee were as follows: KANAZAWA Atsushi, WATANABE Shōgo, Rolf Giebel of New Zealand, and Rudy Smet of Belgium.

After holding planning meetings on a monthly basis, the Committee selected one hundred thirty-nine texts for the First Series of translations, an estimated one hundred printed volumes in all. The texts selected are not necessarily limited to those originally written in India but also include works written or composed in China and Japan. While the publication of the First Series proceeds, the texts for the Second Series will be selected from among the remaining works; this process will continue until all the texts, in Japanese as well as in Chinese, have been published.

Frankly speaking, it will take perhaps one hundred years or more to accomplish the English translation of the complete Chinese and Japanese texts, for they consist of thousands of works. Nevertheless, as Dr. NUMATA wished, it is the sincere hope of the Committee that this project will continue unto completion, even after all its present members have passed away.

It must be mentioned here that the final object of this project is
not academic fulfillment but the transmission of the teaching of the
Buddha to the whole world in order to create harmony and peace
among humankind. To that end, the translators have been asked to
minimize the use of explanatory notes of the kind that are indispen-
sable in academic texts, so that the attention of general readers will
not be unduly distracted from the primary text. Also, a glossary of
selected terms is appended to aid in understanding the text.

To my great regret, however, Dr. NUMATA passed away on May 5,
1994, at the age of ninety-seven, entrusting his son, Mr. NUMATA Toshihide, with the continuation and completion of the Translation Project.
The Committee also lost its able and devoted Chairperson, Professor
HANAYAMA Shōyū, on June 16, 1995, at the age of sixty-three. After
these severe blows, the Committee elected me, then Vice President of
Musashino Women's College, to be the Chair in October 1995. The
Committee has renewed its determination to carry out the noble intention of Dr. NUMATA, under the leadership of Mr. NUMATA Toshihide.

The present members of the Committee are MAYEDA Sengaku
(Chairperson), ISHIGAMI Zennō, ICHISHIMA Shōshin, KANAOKA Shūyū,
NARA Yasuaki, TAMARU Noriyoshi, URYŪZU Ryūshin, YUYAMA Akira,
Kenneth K. Tanaka, WATANABE Shōgo, and assistant member
YONEZAWA Yoshiyasu.

The Numata Center for Buddhist Translation and Research was
established in November 1984, in Berkeley, California, U.S.A., to
assist in the publication of the BDK English Tripiṭaka First Series.
In December 1991, the Publication Committee was organized at the
Numata Center, with Professor Philip Yampolsky as the Chairperson. To our sorrow, Professor Yampolsky passed away in July 1996.
In February 1997, Dr. Kenneth K. Inada became Chair and served
in that capacity until August 1999. The current Chair, Dr. Francis
H. Cook, has been continuing the work since October 1999. All of the
remaining texts will be published under the supervision of this Committee, in close cooperation with the Editorial Committee in Tokyo.

MAYEDA Sengaku
Chairperson
Editorial Committee of
the BDK English Tripiṭaka

Publisher's Foreword

The Publication Committee shares with the Editorial Committee the responsibility of realizing the vision of Dr. Yehan Numata, founder of Bukkyō Dendō Kyōkai, the Society for the Promotion of Buddhism. This vision is no less than to make the Buddha's teaching better known throughout the world, through the translation and publication in English of the entire collection of Buddhist texts compiled in the *Taishō Shinshū Daizōkyō,* published in Tokyo in the early part of the twentieth century. This huge task is expected to be carried out by several generations of translators and may take as long as a hundred years to complete. Ultimately, the entire canon will be available to anyone who can read English and who wishes to learn more about the teaching of the Buddha.

The present generation of staff members of the Publication Committee includes Marianne Dresser; Brian Nagata, president of the Numata Center for Buddhist Translation and Research, Berkeley, California; Eisho Nasu; and Reverend Kiyoshi Yamashita. The Publication Committee is headquartered at the Numata Center and, working in close cooperation with the Editorial Committee, is responsible for the usual tasks associated with preparing translations for publication.

In October 1999, I became the third chairperson of the Publication Committee, on the retirement of its very capable former chair, Dr. Kenneth K. Inada. The Committee is devoted to the advancement of the Buddha's teaching through the publication of excellent translations of the thousands of texts that make up the Buddhist canon.

Francis H. Cook
Chairperson
Publication Committee

Contents

THE SUTRA OF QUEEN ŚRĪMĀLĀ
OF THE LION'S ROAR

Contents

Translator's Introduction

The *Sutra of Queen Śrīmālā of the Lion's Roar* (*Śrīmālādevīsiṁha-nāda-sūtra*) is a Mahayana text no longer extant in Sanskrit but preserved in both the Chinese and Tibetan Buddhist canons. This text is a unique development within the Buddhist tradition because of its egalitarian and generous view concerning women, portraying, on the one hand, the dignity and wisdom of a laywoman and her concern for all beings, and, on the other, the role of woman as philosopher and teacher. The major philosophical emphases of the text are the theories of the "womb of the Buddha" (*tathāgatagarbha*) and the One Vehicle (*ekayāna*).

Because of the number of citations and references that are retained in Sanskrit Buddhist texts, the *Śrīmālādevīsiṁhanāda-sūtra* seems to have been widely circulated at one time throughout India. The Chinese Buddhist canon has preserved two versions of the text: an earlier translation by Guṇabhadra (394–468), from which this English translation has been made, and a later translation by Bodhiruci (672–727).

The story of Queen Śrīmālā has a simple and beautiful theme, full of lush imagery and metaphors. The bodhisattva is the essential agent through whom living beings are instructed in the profound teaching of the *tathāgatagarbha* ("womb of the Buddha"). A future Buddha who is still embracing the teachings and instructing others, Queen Śrīmālā becomes a bodhisattva who explains the doctrine of the *tathāgatagarbha* in the presence of the Buddha, after her parents send her a letter requesting that she study the teaching (Dharma). Awakening to the thought of enlightenment (*bodhicitta*), meditating upon the Buddha, she visualizes him and expresses the wish to follow the bodhisattva path. Receiving the prediction of her

5

future Buddhahood from the Buddha, she enters the path of the True Dharma and thus begins her bodhisattva practice.

Queen Śrīmālā, who had the "lion's roar"—or eloquence—of a Buddha, first converts the women of her kingdom, then her husband, a non-Buddhist, and finally the men. Śrīmālā is praised for her intelligence and compassion, not for her beauty or wealth, which are implicit. She is proficient in explaining the Dharma and is charismatic, as are all the bodhisattvas throughout Buddhist literature. Queen Śrīmālā describes the True Dharma using four metaphors: 1) the great cloud, which is the source of all good merits pouring forth on living beings; 2) the great waters, which are the source for creating all good meritorious acts; 3) the great earth, which carries all things just as the True Dharma supports all living things; and 4) the four jewel storehouses, which are the four types of instructions that living beings accept and embrace.

The text raises the question of the possibility of female Buddhas. This question had continually vexed Buddhist scholars and commentators, who attempted to come to terms with the possibility of a relationship between the notion of the ultimate spiritual perfection or Buddhahood and the feminine. Such a relationship was viewed with ambivalence. This question was raised only by Mahayana Buddhists, particularly those who proclaimed the one path to universal Buddhahood. For these Buddhists, all men and women equally had the nature of the Buddha. If women were truly capable of having Buddha-nature in this lifetime without denying their female gender, this would implicitly indicate that women were not biologically determined as religiously, psychologically, and physically inferior to men.

One popular theme in Mahayana Buddhist texts had been the teaching of transformation from female to male, providing a means, both literary and spiritual, for women to become bodhisattvas and Buddhas. Other texts and commentaries suggest that there is no need to undergo a gender change through either vowing to despise the female nature or through rebirth as a male after death as a female.

The controversy that arose among scholars concerning Queen Śrīmālā's level of spiritual attainment may reflect continual controversy among Buddhists with regard to the bodhisattva ideal and the image of Buddhahood as female.

The entire tone of the text, in which the bodhisattva is the supporter, acceptor, and compassionate Dharma mother, suggests female imagery. The question of whether or not women were ever recognized as potential or imminent Buddhas remains unanswered.

THE TEACHING OF QUEEN ŚRĪMĀLĀ
OF THE LION'S ROAR

A comprehensive text that teaches the skillful means
of the One Vehicle. Translated from the Sanskrit by the
Central Indian Tripiṭaka Master Guṇabhadra in 435 C.E.

Chapter I

The Merits of the Tathāgata's True Dharma

Thus have I heard. One time the Buddha was residing in the Jeta Garden of Anāthapiṇḍika's Park in the city of Śrāvastī [in the kingdom of Kosala]. At that time King Prasenajit and Queen Mallikā, who had only recently attained faith in the Dharma, said these words together, "Śrīmālā, our daughter, is astute and extremely intelligent. If she has the opportunity to see the Buddha, she will certainly understand the Dharma without doubting [its truth]. Some time we should send a message to her to awaken her religious state of mind."

The queen said, "Now is the right time." The king and queen then wrote a letter to Śrīmālā, praising the Tathāgata's immeasurable merits, and dispatched a messenger named Candirā to deliver the letter to the kingdom of Ayodhyā [where Śrīmālā was queen]. Entering the palace, the messenger respectfully conferred the letter to Śrīmālā who rejoiced upon receiving it, raising the letter to her head [as a sign of reverence]. She read and understood it, arousing a religious mind of rare quality. Then she said to Candirā in verse:

"I hear the name 'Buddha,'
The One who is rarely in the world.
If my words are true [that the Buddha is now in the world]
Then I will honor him.

"Since I humbly submit that the Lord Buddha
Came for the sake of the world,
He should be compassionate with me
Allowing me to see him."

11

At that very moment of reflection,
The Buddha appeared in heaven,
Radiating pure light in all directions,
And revealing his incomparable body.

Śrīmālā and her attendants
Prostrated themselves reverently at his feet,
And with pure minds,
Praised the true merits of the Buddha:

"The body of the Tathāgata, excellent in form,
Is unequaled in the world,
Being incomparable and inconceivable.
Therefore, we now honor you.

"The Tathāgata's form is inexhaustible
And likewise his wisdom.
All things eternally abide [in him].
Therefore, we take refuge in you.

"Having already exorcised the mind's defilements
And the four kinds [of faults] of body [and speech]
You have already arrived at the undaunted stage.
Therefore we worship you, the Dharma King.

217b

"By knowing all objects to be known,
And by the self-mastery of your body of wisdom,
You encompass all things.
Therefore, we now honor you.

"We honor you, the One who transcends all measures
    [of space and time].
We honor you, the One who is incomparable.
We honor you, the One who has the limitless Dharma.
We honor you, the One beyond conceptualization."

[Śrīmālā:]

"Please be compassionate and protect me,

12

Causing the seeds of Dharma to grow [within me]
In this life and in future lives,
Please, Buddha, always accept me."

[The Buddha:]

"I have been with you for a long time,
Guiding you in former lives.
I now again accept you.
And will do likewise in the future."

[Śrīmālā:]

"I have produced merits
At present and in other lives.
Because of these virtuous deeds
I only wish to be accepted."

Then Śrīmālā and all of her attendants prostrated themselves before the Buddha's feet. The Buddha then made this prediction among them:

"You praise the true merits of the Tathāgata because of your virtuous deeds. After immeasurable periods of time, you will become sovereign among the gods (*devas*). In all lives you will continually see me and praise me in my presence, in the same manner as you are doing now. You will also make offerings to the immeasurable numbers of Buddhas for more than twenty thousand immeasurable periods of time. Then you (Śrīmālā) will become the Buddha named Universal Light (Samantaprabha), the Tathāgata, Arhat, Perfectly Enlightened One. Your Buddha land will have no evil destinies and no suffering due to old age, illness, deterioration, torments.... There will be no evil whatsoever, not even the word for evil. Those who are in your land will have the five desires [of the senses fulfilled], longevity, physical power, and physical beauty, and will be happier than even the gods who control enjoyments created by others. They all will be exclusively Mahayana, having habitually practiced virtuous deeds, and assembling in your land."

When Queen Śrīmālā had received this prediction, the innumerable gods, humans, and other beings vowed to be born in her land. The Buddha predicted to everyone that they all would be born there.

Chapter II

The Ten Ordination Vows

At that time Śrīmālā, having received the [Buddha's] prediction, respectfully arose to take the ten major ordination vows.

"O Lord, from now until I am enlightened:

1) "I will not transgress the discipline that I have received.

2) "I will have no disrespect toward the venerable elders.

3) "I will not hate living beings.

4) "I will not be jealous of others with regard to either their   217c physical appearance or their possessions.

5) "I will not be stingy although I have little sustenance.

"O Lord, from now until I am enlightened:

6) "I will not accumulate property for my own benefit. Whatever I receive will be used to assist living beings who are poor and suffering.

7) "I will practice the four all-embracing acts (giving, kind speech, benefiting others, and cooperation toward leading all beings to virtuous deeds) for all living beings, and not for myself. I accept all living beings without lust, without satiation, and without prejudice.

8) "When I see living beings who are lonely, imprisoned, ill, and afflicted by various misfortunes and hardships, I will never forsake them, even for a moment, for I must bring them peace. Through my good deeds I will bring them benefits and liberate them from their pain. Only then will I leave them.

9) "When I see those who hunt or domesticate animals, slaughter, or commit other such offenses against the precepts, I will never forsake them. When I obtain this power [to teach all beings], I will restrain those who should be restrained and assist those who should be assisted wherever I see such living beings. Why? Because by

restraining and assisting them, one causes the eternal continuation of the Dharma. If the Dharma continues eternally, gods and humans shall flourish and the evil destinies shall diminish in number. Then the wheel of the Dharma that is turned by the Tathāgata will again be turned. Because I see these benefits I will save, and never quit [teaching living beings].

"O Lord, from now until I am enlightened:

10) "I accept the True Dharma, never forgetting it. Why? Because those who forget the Dharma forget the Mahayana. Those who forget the Mahayana forget the perfections (*pāramitās*). Those who forget the perfections do not aspire toward the Mahayana. If the bodhisattvas are not committed to the Mahayana, they cannot have the aspiration to accept the True Dharma. Acting according to their pleasure, they will not be able to transcend the level of common people.

"Because I have seen, in this way, the immeasurably great errors [of humans] and have seen the immeasurable merits of the bodhisattvas, those great beings (*mahāsattvas*) who will accept the True Dharma, I will accept these great ordination vows.

"O Lord of the Dharma manifested before me, you are my witness. Even though the Lord Buddha presently witnessed [my testimony], living beings' virtuous deeds are superficial. Some of them are skeptical and extremely difficult to save through these ten ordination vows. They engage in immoral activities for long periods of time and are unhappy. In order to bring peace to them, I now declare, in your presence, that my vows are sincere.

"If I receive these ten major ordination vows and practice them as I have stated them, by [the power of] these true words, heavenly flowers will rain down and divine music will ring out upon this assembly."

Just as Śrīmālā said these words, a shower of heavenly flowers poured from the sky and divine music rang out: "It is so! It is so! What you have said is true, not false." Having seen these wondrous flowers and having heard this music, the entire assembly no longer was skeptical, rejoicing immeasurably and exclaiming,

218a

"We wish to stay with Queen Śrīmālā and together we would like to join in practice with her."

The Buddha predicted to all that their wish [to stay with Queen Śrīmālā] would be fulfilled.

Chapter III

The Three Great Vows

At that time Śrīmālā again, in the presence of the Buddha, professed the three great vows:

"By the power of my earnest aspiration, may I bring peace to innumerable and unlimited living beings. By my virtuous deeds, throughout all rebirths may I attain the wisdom of the True Dharma." This is called the first great vow.

"Having attained the wisdom of the True Dharma, for the sake of all living beings, may I explain [the Dharma] without wearying." This is called the second great vow.

"In accepting the True Dharma, may I abandon body, life, and wealth and uphold the True Dharma." This is called the third great vow.

At that time the Lord prophesied to Śrīmālā, "With reference to the three great vows, just as all forms are contained in space, so likewise the bodhisattva vows, which are as numerous as the sands of the Ganges River, are all contained in these three great vows. These three vows are the truth and are extensive."

Chapter IV

Acceptance of the True Dharma

At that time Queen Śrīmālā said to the Buddha, "Having received the Buddha's power, I will now explain the great vow which is controlled [by the principle of the True Dharma], being the truth without error."

The Buddha said to Śrīmālā, "I permit you to explain as you wish."

Śrīmālā said to the Buddha, "The bodhisattva vows, which are as numerous as the sands of the Ganges River, are all contained in the one great vow that is called 'acceptance of the True Dharma.' Acceptance of the True Dharma truly is the great vow."

The Buddha praised Śrīmālā: "Excellent! Excellent! Your wisdom (*prajñā*) and skillful means (*upāya*) are most profound and subtle! You have already, for a long time, increased in virtue. In the future, living beings who develop such virtue will be able to understand you. Your explanation of the acceptance of the True Dharma is that which the Buddhas of the past, present, and future have explained, now explain, and will explain. Having realized supreme, complete enlightenment (*anuttarā samyaksaṃbodhi*), I also speak of this acceptance of the True Dharma. I explain that acceptance of the True Dharma has merits that cannot be limited. The Tathāgata's wisdom and eloquence also are without limits. Why? Because in this acceptance of the True Dharma there are great merits and great benefits."

Queen Śrīmālā said to the Buddha, "Again, having received the Buddha's power, I shall further explain the extension of the acceptance of the True Dharma."

The Buddha said, "Then please explain."

1. Immeasurable

A. Like a Great Cloud

Śrīmālā said to the Buddha, "The meaning of the extension of the acceptance of the True Dharma is immeasurable. It includes all teachings of the Buddha, consisting of eighty-four thousand discourses.

218b
"Like a great cloud that appeared at the time of creation, showering down multicolored rain and many kinds of jewels, acceptance of the True Dharma rains forth innumerable rewards and innumerable virtues."

B. Like the Great Waters

"O Lord, at the time of creation, the three thousand great worlds and the forty billion kinds of continents emerged from the great waters. Similarly, the innumerable worlds of the Mahayana, the supernatural powers of all the bodhisattvas, the peace and happiness of all worlds, the magical omnipotence of all worlds, and the peace of the transcendental worlds that has not been experienced by gods and humans from the time of creation—all these emerge from acceptance of the True Dharma."

C. Like the Great Earth, the "Supporter"

"Moreover, acceptance of the True Dharma is like the great earth that supports four weights. What are the four? The great seas, the mountains, vegetation, and living beings. Similarly, like that great earth, good sons and daughters who accept the True Dharma build the great earth and carry four responsibilities. Who are the four? 1) Living beings who have parted from good friends either have not heard [the Dharma] or are without the Dharma. By advising them to cultivate the good deeds of humans and gods, [good sons and daughters] prepare them [for entering the path]. 2) For those who want to be disciples (*śrāvaka*s) they present the disciple vehicle. 3) For those who want to be *pratyekabuddhas* (solitary enlightened ones) they present the *pratyekabuddha* vehicle. And 4) for those who want to be [followers of the Great Vehicle], they present the Mahayana. These are the good sons and good daughters who accept the True Dharma, build the great earth, and carry the four responsibilities.

"Therefore, Lord, good sons and daughters who accept the True Dharma, build the great earth, and carry the four responsibilities become friends without being asked for the sake of all living beings. In their great compassion, they comfort and sympathize with living beings and become the Dharma mother of the world."

2. Like the Great Earth, Which Has Four Jewel Storehouses

"Again, acceptance of the True Dharma is like the great earth that has four kinds of jewel storehouses. What are the four? They are: 1) the priceless, 2) the supremely valuable, 3) the moderately valuable, and 4) the slightly valuable. These are the great earth's four kinds of jewel storehouses.

"Similarly, good sons and daughters who accept the True Dharma and build the great earth obtain the four kinds of most precious jewels, namely, living beings. Who are the four? 1) Those who have not heard [the Dharma] or are without the Dharma to whom the good sons and daughters who have accepted the True Dharma present the [cultivation of] merits and virtuous deeds of humans and gods. 2) Those who want to be disciples are presented with the disciple vehicle. 3) Those who want to be *pratyekabuddhas* are presented with the *pratyekabuddha* vehicle. And 4) those who want to [follow the Great Vehicle] are presented with the Mahayana.

"Therefore, all the good sons and daughters who obtain the great jewels, namely living beings, realize extraordinarily rare merits because of acceptance of the Dharma. Lord, the great jewel storehouse is the acceptance of the True Dharma."

3. Identical with the True Dharma Itself

"Lord, 'acceptance of the True Dharma' means the True Dharma [itself] is not different from acceptance of the True Dharma. The True Dharma [itself] is identical with acceptance of the True Dharma."

4. Identical with the Perfections

218c "Lord, the perfections are not different from the one who accepts the True Dharma. The one who accepts the True Dharma is identical with the perfections. Why?

1) "Good sons and daughters who accept the True Dharma give even their body and limbs for those who respond to giving. By protecting these [living beings'] intentions, they teach them. When they are thus taught and caused to abide in the True Dharma, this is called the perfection of giving (dāna).

2) "Good sons and daughters teach the protection of the six senses, the purification of body, speech, and mind, and the cultivation of the four correct postures [in walking, standing, sitting, and reclining] to those who respond to discipline. By protecting these [living beings'] intentions, they teach them. When they are thus taught and caused to abide in the True Dharma, this is called the perfection of discipline (śīla).

3) "Good sons and daughters teach nonhatred, supreme patience, and neutrality in outer expression to those who respond to patience. By protecting these [living beings'] intentions, they teach them. When they are thus taught and caused to abide in the True Dharma, this is called the perfection of patience (kṣānti).

4) "Good sons and daughters do not teach indolence but the desire [to practice], supreme perseverance, and cultivation of the four correct postures to those who respond to perseverance. By protecting these [living beings'] intentions, they teach them. When they are thus taught and caused to abide in the True Dharma, this is called the perfection of perseverance (vīrya).

5) "Good sons and daughters teach tranquility, constant mindfulness not conditioned by external objects, and recollection of all actions and speech over long periods of time to those who respond to meditation. By protecting these [living beings'] intentions, they teach them. When they are thus taught and caused to abide in the True Dharma, this is called the perfection of meditation (*dhyāna*).

6) "Good sons and daughters, when questioned concerning the meaning of all things, extensively teach all treatises and all arts, without trepidation, causing those who respond to wisdom to reach the ultimate in science and art. By protecting these [living beings'] intentions, they teach them. When they are thus taught and caused to abide in the True Dharma, this is the perfection of wisdom (*prajñā*).

"Therefore, O Lord, the perfections are not different from the one who accepts the True Dharma. The one who accepts the True Dharma is identical with the perfections.

"O Lord, now receiving your power, I will further explain the greatness [of the True Dharma]."

The Buddha said, "Please do so."

[Identical with the One Who Accepts the True Dharma]

Śrīmālā said to the Buddha, "'Acceptance of the True Dharma' means acceptance of the True Dharma is not different from the one who accepts the True Dharma. Good sons and daughters who accept the True Dharma are identical with acceptance of the True Dharma. Why? Because good sons and daughters who accept the True Dharma abandon three things for the sake of acceptance of the True Dharma. What are the three? They are body, life, and wealth.

219a

"When good sons and daughters abandon the body, they become equal to the last limit of the cycle of birth and death (samsara). Having parted from old age, illness, and death, they realize the indestructible, eternal, unchanging, and inconceivable merits of the Tathāgata's Dharma body (*dharmakāya*).

"When they abandon life, they become equal to the last limit of the cycle of birth and death. Ultimately, having parted from death, they realize the limitless, eternal, and inconceivable merits, penetrating all the profound Buddha-Dharmas.

"When they abandon property, they become equal to the last limit of the cycle of birth and death. Having realized the inexhaustible, indestructible, ultimately eternal, inconceivable, and complete merits that are not common to all other living beings, they obtain the excellent offerings of all living beings.

"Lord, good sons and daughters who have abandoned these three (body, life, and wealth) and have accepted the True Dharma will always obtain the predictions of all the Buddhas [concerning their Buddhahood], and will be honored by all living beings.

"Furthermore, O Lord, good sons and daughters who accept the True Dharma without distortion, and without deception or misrepresentation, will love the True Dharma and accept the True Dharma, entering into Dharma friendship when the [four groups of followers] (monks, nuns, laymen, and laywomen) are forming rival factions that cause the destruction and dispersion [of the sangha]. Those who enter into Dharma friendship will certainly receive the prediction [of their future Buddhahood] by all the Buddhas.

"O Lord, I see that acceptance of the True Dharma has such great powers. Because you are the eye of truth, the wisdom of truth, the source of the Dharma, and you penetrate all things, you are the basis for the True Dharma and know all things."

At that time, the Lord was joyous over Śrīmālā's explanation concerning the great powers of acceptance of the True Dharma. [The Buddha said,] "Śrīmālā, what you have said is true. The great powers of acceptance of the True Dharma are like a very strong man who only briefly touches a [vulnerable] part of one's body yet causes great pain. Similarly, Śrīmālā, barely accepting the True Dharma causes suffering to Māra, the Evil One. I do not see even one remaining good act that can cause suffering to Māra in the manner that only barely accepting the True Dharma does.

"Moreover, the bull king has a form without equal, surpassing all other bulls. Similarly, even just barely accepting the True Dharma in the Mahayana is superior to all the virtuous deeds of the two vehicles, because it is so extensive.

"The majestic bearing and uniqueness of great Mount Sumeru surpasses all other mountains. Similarly, the [merit of] abandonment of body, life, and wealth in the Mahayana, acceptance of the True Dharma with a benevolent heart, surpasses [the merit of] those who have engaged only in the virtuous deeds of the Mahayana but do not abandon body, life, and wealth. Because of its extensiveness, of course it is superior to the two vehicles.

"Thus, Śrīmālā, through acceptance of the True Dharma, explain [this teaching] to living beings, teach and convert living beings, and confirm living beings [in the Dharma].

"Therefore, Śrīmālā, acceptance of the True Dharma has these great benefits, these great blessings, and these great fruits. Śrīmālā, even if I explain the merits and benefits of acceptance of the True Dharma for countless periods of time, I shall not reach the end [of explaining it]. Therefore, acceptance of the True Dharma has immeasurable and unlimited merits."

219b

Chapter V

The One Vehicle

The Buddha said to Queen Śrīmālā, "Now you should further explain the acceptance of the True Dharma that was taught by all the Buddhas."

Queen Śrīmālā said to the Buddha, "Very well, O Lord, I will, upon receiving your exhortation." Then she said to the Buddha, "O Lord, acceptance of the True Dharma is [acceptance of] the Mahayana. Why? Because the Mahayana brings forth all the good acts of the world and of the transcendental, of the disciples and of the *pratyekabuddha*s. O Lord, just as the eight great rivers flow from Lake Anavatapta, so likewise all the good acts of the world and of the transcendental, of the disciples and of the *pratyekabuddha*s, emerge from the Mahayana.

"O Lord, moreover, just as all seeds are able to grow [only] when they depend upon the earth, so likewise all the good acts of the world, of the transcendental, of the disciples, and of the *pratyekabuddha*s are able to increase [only] when they depend upon the Mahayana. Therefore, O Lord, abiding in the Mahayana, one accepts Mahayana—this is identical with abiding in the two vehicles and accepting all the good acts of the world, of the transcendental, and of the two vehicles.

"What are the six stations that the Lord explains? They are: 1) the continuity of the True Dharma, 2) the extinction of the True Dharma, 3) the rules of the *Prātimokṣa*, 4) the discipline of the Vinaya, 5) renunciation of one's home, and 6) ordination. On behalf of the Mahayana, the Lord preaches these six stations. Why? Because the continuity of the True Dharma is explained for the sake of the Mahayana. Continuity of the Mahayana is continuity of the True Dharma. Extinction of the Mahayana is extinction of the True Dharma.

"The rules of the *Prātimokṣa* and the discipline of the Vinaya have the same meaning even though they are different in name. The discipline of the Vinaya is learned by Mahayanists. Why? Because one renounces home and becomes ordained for the sake of the Buddha. Therefore, the conduct of the Mahayana, which is the [perfection of] discipline, is the Vinaya—renouncing one's home and taking ordination.

"Consequently, in the case of the arhat, there is no renunciation of home nor taking ordination [as a separate vehicle from the Mahayana]. Why? Because the arhat renounces his home and is ordained for the sake of the Tathāgata. The arhat, seeking refuge in the Buddha, is afraid. Why? Because the arhat lives in a state of fear toward all conditioning forces, as if a man holding a sword wished to cause him harm. Therefore, the arhat has no ultimate happiness. Why? O Lord, being a [final] refuge, one does not seek refuge. Living beings who are without a refuge, having this or that fear, seek refuge because of these fears. Likewise, arhats who have fears seek refuge in the Tathāgata because of these fears.

219c "O Lord, arhats and *pratyekabuddhas* are afraid. Because these arhats and *pratyekabuddhas* still have not extinguished their lives, these [psychophysical forces] continue. They have not completed the practice of purity, and so remain impure. Because their actions are not ultimate, they still have actions to perform. Because they have not reached that [final stage], they still have defilements that should be severed. Because these are not severed, one is far from the realm of nirvana. Why? Because only the Tathāgata, Arhat, Perfectly Enlightened One attains final nirvana, being endowed with all merits. Arhats and *pratyekabuddhas* are not endowed with all merits. When it is said that they attain nirvana, this is [merely] the skillful means of the Buddha.

"Because only the Tathāgata attains final nirvana, being endowed with inconceivable merits, arhats and *pratyekabuddhas* are only endowed with conceivable merits. When it is said that they attain nirvana, this is [merely] the skillful means of the Buddha.

"Because only the Tathāgata attains final nirvana, eliminating transgressions that should be eliminated and endowed with supreme purity, arhats and *pratyekabuddha*s who still have transgressions are not supremely pure. When it is said that they attain nirvana, this is [merely] the skillful means of the Buddha.

"Only the Tathāgata attains final nirvana, is revered by all living beings, and surpasses the arhat, *pratyekabuddha,* and bodhisattva realms. Therefore, arhats and *pratyekabuddha*s are far from the realm of nirvana. When it is said that the arhats and *pratyekabuddha*s meditate on liberation, have the four wisdoms, and have ultimately attained their resting place, this is also the skillful means of the Tathāgata and is taught as the incomplete meaning. Why? There are two kinds of death. What are the two? They are ordinary death and the inconceivable death of transformation [for a purpose]. Ordinary death refers to living beings who live in unreality. The inconceivable death of transformation [for a purpose] refers to the mind-made bodies of the arhats, *pratyekabuddha*s, and greatly powerful bodhisattvas until the time of their supreme, complete enlightenment.

"Within these two kinds of death, it is the ordinary death through which arhats and *pratyekabuddha*s have completely attained the knowledge said to have 'extinguished their lives.' Because they attain realization (nirvana) with remainder, it is said that 'the practice of holiness has been completely upheld.' Because their errors and defilements have been eliminated, it is said that 'their actions have been completed,' actions which the common people, gods, and seven kinds of educated people are incapable of performing. Because arhats and *pratyekabuddha*s cannot be reborn since their defilements are eliminated, it is said that 'they are not reborn.' When it is said that 'they are not reborn,' this is not because they have eliminated *all* defilements nor exhausted *all* births. Why? Because there are defilements that cannot be eliminated by arhats and *pratyekabuddha*s. 220a

31

"There are two kinds of defilements. What are the two? They are latent defilements and active defilements. There are four kinds of latent defilements. They are: 1) the stage of all [false] views of monism, 2) the stage of desiring sense pleasures, 3) the stage of desiring forms, and 4) the stage of desiring existence. From these four stages of [defilement], there are all the active defilements. 'What is active' is momentary and associated with the momentariness of the mind. O Lord, the mind does not associate with the stage of beginningless ignorance [in the same manner].

"O Lord, the power of these four latent defilements is a basis for all active defilements but cannot possibly be compared in number, fraction, counting, similarity, nor resemblance to ignorance [in power].

"O Lord, such is the power of the stage of ignorance! The power of the stage of ignorance is much greater than the other stages represented by the fourth stage of desire for existence. The power of the stage of ignorance is like that of the wicked Evil One (Māra), whose form, power, longevity, and retainers are both superior to and more powerful than the heaven where the gods control the enjoyments created by others. Its power is far superior to that of the other stages of defilement represented by the fourth stage of desire for existence. This basis for the active defilements, more numerous than the sands of the Ganges River, causes the four kinds of defilements to continue for a long time. The arhats' and *pratyekabuddhas*' wisdom cannot eliminate it. Only the Tathāgata's enlightenment-wisdom can eliminate it. Yes, O Lord, the stage of ignorance is extremely powerful!

"O Lord, the three states of existence arise, conditioned by clinging to existence and by defiled actions. In like manner, O Lord, the three forms of mind-made bodies of arhats, *pratyekabuddhas*, and greatly powerful bodhisattvas are conditioned by the stage of ignorance and by pure actions. In these three levels (the arhat, *pratyekabuddha*, and bodhisattva stages), the three kinds of mind-made bodies and pure actions are based upon the latent stage of ignorance. Because all things are conditioned and not unconditioned, the three kinds of mind-made bodies and pure actions are conditioned by the stage of ignorance.

"O Lord, thus the other stages of defilement, represented by the fourth stage of desire for existence, are not identical with the stage of ignorance with respect to action. The stage of ignorance is different from the four stages and is eliminated by the Buddha stages and by the enlightenment-wisdom of the Buddha. Why? Arhats and *pratyekabuddhas* eliminate the four kinds of stages but their purity is not complete, for they have not attained autonomy nor have they accomplished their realization [of enlightenment].

"'Their purity that is not completed' refers to the stage of ignorance. O Lord, arhats, *pratyekabuddhas*, and bodhisattvas in their very last body do not know and do not awaken to the various phenomena because of the impediments of the stage of ignorance. Because they are not aware [of these phenomena] they cannot absolutely eliminate what should be eliminated. Because they do not eliminate [all defilements] they are 'liberated with remaining faults,' which is not 'liberation separated from all faults.' They have 'purity with remaining' [purification to be done,] which is not purity in its entirety. They 'accomplish merits with remaining' [merits to be accomplished,] which is not entirely meritorious. Because they accomplish liberation with remainder, purity with remainder, and merits with remainder, arhats, *pratyekabuddhas*, and bodhisattvas know suffering with remainder, eliminate the source of suffering with remainder, attain the extinction of suffering with remainder, and practice the path with remainder. This is 'attaining partial nirvana.' 220b

"Those who attain partial nirvana are 'turned toward the nirvana realm.' If one knows all suffering, entirely eliminates the source of suffering, attains the complete extinction [of suffering], and practices the entire path, one will attain permanent nirvana in a world that is impermanent and decadent, impermanent and distressed. In a world without protection, a world without a refuge, there is a protector and a refuge. Why? There is attainment of nirvana because of [the differentiation between] inferior and superior phenomena. [O Lord, there is attainment of nirvana because of the equality of all phenomena.] Because of the equality of knowledge, one attains nirvana. Because of the equality of liberation, one attains nirvana. Because of the equality of purity, one attains nirvana. Therefore, nirvana has the same quality as liberation.

O Lord, if the stage of ignorance is not absolutely eliminated, then one does not attain the same quality of knowledge and liberation. Why? If the stage of ignorance is not absolutely eliminated, then phenomena more numerous than the sands of the Ganges River that should be eliminated will not be absolutely eliminated. Because phenomena more numerous than the sands of the Ganges River that should be eliminated are not eliminated, the phenomena more numerous than the sands of the Ganges River that should be attained will not be attained, and [the phenomena] that should be manifested will not be manifested. Therefore, the accumulation [of defilements] in the stage of ignorance produces both the defilements that are severed by the practice of the entire path and the virulent defilements, as well as the virulent defilements of the mind, of meditation, of concentration, of contemplation, of insight, of skillful means, of wisdom, of the results [of the path], of attainment, of power, and of fearlessness. These are all the active defilements more numerous than the sands of the Ganges River that are eliminated by the enlightenment-wisdom of the Tathāgata.

"All these defilements are due to the stage of ignorance. All the active defilements that arise are caused by and conditioned by the stage of ignorance. O Lord, among the defilements that arise, the mind and its various faculties arise together momentarily. O Lord, the mind does not associate with the stage of beginningless ignorance [in the same manner].

"O Lord, all phenomena more numerous than the sands of the Ganges River that should be eliminated by the Tathāgata's enlightenment-wisdom are supported and sustained by the stage of ignorance. For example, all the seeds that depend on the earth for their life, sustenance, and growth would be ruined if the earth were ruined. Similarly, all phenomena more numerous than the sands of the Ganges River that should be eliminated by the Tathāgata's enlightenment-wisdom are based upon the stage of ignorance for their life, sustenance, and growth.

"If the stage of ignorance is eliminated, all phenomena more numerous than the sands of the Ganges River that should be elim- 220c inated by the Tathāgata's enlightenment-wisdom will be eliminated. If all defilements and virulent defilements are eliminated, all phenomena more numerous than the sands of the Ganges River will be attained by the Tathāgatas, who penetrate them without obstruction. Omniscience is separate from all transgressions, attaining all the merits of the Dharma King, the Dharma Lord, attaining autonomy and manifesting the stage of autonomy from all phenomena.

"O Tathāgata, Arhat, Perfectly Enlightened One, who has the lion's roar, the complete extinction of one's life, 'the complete practice of holiness,' 'the completion of actions,' and the 'nonacceptance of rebirth' have been explained up until now, based upon your lion's roar, for their complete meaning.

"O Lord, there are two kinds of knowledge that do not accept rebirth. First, there is the knowledge of the Tathāgatas who, by means of their unsurpassed powers, subdue the four Evil Ones, appear in all worlds, and are worshiped by all living beings. They attain the inconceivable Dharma body, all spheres of knowledge, and unobstructed autonomy in all things. In this stage there is no action nor attainment that is higher. Having the ten magnificent powers [of knowledge] they ascend to the supreme, unexcelled, fearless stage. With their omniscient, unobstructed knowledge, they understand without relying on another. This wisdom that does not accept rebirth is the lion's roar.

"O Lord, second, there is the knowledge of arhats and *pratyeka-buddhas* who cross over the fears of birth and death and gradually attain the happiness of liberation with this thought: 'I have parted from the fears of birth and death and no longer experience the suffering of birth and death.' Lord, when arhats and *pratyekabuddhas* meditate, they do not accept rebirth and have insight into the supremely restful stage of nirvana.

"O Lord, those who first attained that stage [of nirvana] were not ignorant of the Dharma and were not dependent upon others. They also knew they had attained the stages with remainder [through their own efforts], and would inevitably attain supreme, complete enlightenment (*anuttarā samyaksaṃbodhi*). Why? Because the *śrāvaka* (disciple) and *pratyekabuddha* vehicles are included in the Mahayana. The Mahayana is the Buddha vehicle. Therefore, the three vehicles are the One Vehicle.

"Those who attain the One Vehicle attain supreme, complete enlightenment. Supreme, complete enlightenment is the realm of nirvana. The realm of nirvana is the Dharma body of the Tathāgata. Attaining the absolute Dharma body is [attaining] the absolute One Vehicle. The Tathāgata is not different from the Dharma body. The Tathāgata is identical to the Dharma body. If one attains the absolute Dharma body then one attains the absolute One Vehicle. The absolute [One Vehicle] is unlimited and unceasing.

"O Lord, the Tathāgata, who is not limited by time, is the Tathāgata, Arhat, Perfectly Enlightened One, equal to the utmost limit [of the cycle of birth and death]. The Tathāgata is without limitation. His great compassion also is unlimited, bringing peace and comfort to the world. His unlimited great compassion brings unlimited peace and comfort to the world. This explanation is a good explanation concerning the Tathāgata. If one again speaks of the inexhaustible Dharma, the eternally abiding Dharma that is the refuge of all worlds—this is also a good explanation concerning the Tathāgata. Therefore, in a world that has not been saved, a world without a refuge, there is an inexhaustible, eternally abiding refuge equal to the utmost limit [of the cycle of birth and death], namely, the Tathāgata, Arhat, Perfectly Enlightened One.

221a

"The Dharma is the path of the One Vehicle. The sangha is the assembly of the three vehicles. These two refuges are not the ultimate refuge. They are called 'the partial refuge.' Why? The Dharma of the path of the One Vehicle attains the absolute Dharma body. Furthermore, there can be no Dharma body other than that of the One Vehicle.

"The assembly of the three vehicles (the sangha), being afraid, seeks refuge in the Tathāgata. Those students who go out to practice turn toward supreme, complete enlightenment. Therefore, these two refuges are not the ultimate refuge but are limited refuges.

"If there are living beings who are subdued by the Tathāgata, they will seek refuge in the Tathāgata, attain the permeation of the Dharma, and will have faith and happiness, seeking refuge in the Dharma and Sangha. These two refuges, [however,] are not two refuges, for they seek refuge in the Tathāgata. Seeking refuge in the supreme truth is seeking refuge in the Tathāgata.

"The supreme truth of these two refuges is the ultimate refuge, the Tathāgata. Why? Because the Tathāgata is not different from the two refuges. The Tathāgata is identical with the three refuges. Why? Because of the path of the One Vehicle. The Tathāgata, who has perfected the four states of fearlessness, is the one who teaches with the lion's roar. The Tathāgata, according to individual dispositions, teaches through skillful means. This is the Mahayana and not the three vehicles. The three vehicles enter the One Vehicle. The One Vehicle is the supreme vehicle."

Chapter VI

The Unlimited Noble Truths

"O Lord, the disciples and *pratyekabuddha*s first saw the noble truths with their one knowledge that eliminates the latent stages [of defilement]. With their one knowledge, one of the four wisdoms, they eliminate [the source of suffering, namely, the four latent stages of defilements]; know [suffering]; practice virtue [according to the path]; and realize [extinction]. They understand these four [noble truths] very well. O Lord, they do not have the most supreme transcendental wisdom but are gradually reaching the four wisdoms and the four conditions (i.e., the four noble truths). The Dharma that is not gradually reached is supreme transcendental wisdom. O Lord, supreme wisdom is like a diamond.

"O Lord, the disciples and *pratyekabuddha*s do not eliminate the stage of beginningless ignorance. Their initial wisdom of the noble truths is [not] supreme wisdom. Lord, because they do not have the wisdom of the two kinds of noble truths, they eliminate [only] the latent stages [of defilement]. O Lord, the Tathāgata, Arhat, Perfectly Enlightened One is not the realm of all the disciples and *pratyekabuddha*s.

"The inconceivable wisdom of emptiness eliminates the stores of all defilements. O Lord, the ultimate wisdom that destroys the stores of all defilements is called supreme wisdom. The initial wisdom of the noble truths is not ultimate wisdom but is the wisdom that is turned toward supreme, complete enlightenment. 221b

"O Lord, the meaning of 'noble' does not refer to all the disciples and *pratyekabuddha*s. Because the disciples and *pratyekabuddha*s have perfected limited merits and have perfected 'partial' merits, they are called 'noble.' The 'noble truths' are not the

39

truths of the disciples and *pratyekabuddha*s nor are they the merits of the disciples and *pratyekabuddha*s.

"O Lord, these truths are those originally known by the Tathāgata, Arhat, Perfectly Enlightened One. Later, on behalf of the world, which is the womb of ignorance, he appeared to extensively teach what are known as the 'noble truths.'"

Chapter VII

The *Tathāgatagarbha*

"The 'noble truths' have a most profound meaning, which is extremely subtle, difficult to know, and not of the cognitive and finite realms. What is known by those who have this wisdom is inconceivable to the entire world. Why? Because this [profound meaning of the noble truths] explains the most profound *tathā-gatagarbha*. The *tathāgatagarbha* is the realm of the Tathāgata, which is not known by all the disciples and *pratyekabuddhas*. The *tathāgatagarbha* explains the meaning of the noble truths. Because the *tathāgatagarbha* is most profound, explaining the noble truths also is most profound, extremely subtle, difficult to know, and not of the cognitive and finite realms. What is known by those who have this wisdom is inconceivable to the entire world."

Chapter VIII

The Dharma Body

If there are no doubts with reference to the *tathāgatagarbha* that is concealed by the innumerable stores of defilement, then there also will be no doubts with reference to the Dharma body that transcends the innumerable stores of defilement. In explaining the *tathāgatagarbha*, one explains the Dharma body of the Tathāgata, the inconceivable Buddha realms, and skillful means.

"The mind that attains this determination then believes and understands the twofold noble truths. Likewise, what is difficult to know and to understand is the meaning of the twofold noble truths. What is their meaning? They are referred to as the 'conditioned' noble truths and the 'unconditioned' noble truths.

"The 'conditioned' noble truths are the 'limited' four noble truths. Why? Because one who depends on others cannot know all suffering, eliminate all sources of suffering, realize all extinctions of suffering, and practice the entire path. Therefore, O Lord, the cycle of birth and death is both conditioned and unconditioned; nirvana likewise is [conditioned and unconditioned], being [nirvana] with remainder (conditioned) and [nirvana] without remainder (unconditioned).

"The 'unconditioned' noble truths are the 'unlimited' four noble truths. Why? With his own power, one [who knows the unlimited noble truths] can know all suffering, sever all sources of suffering, realize all extinctions of suffering, and practice the entire path.

"These, then, are the eight noble truths. The Tathāgatas taught the four [conditioned] noble truths [as skillful means]. The meaning of the four unconditioned noble truths are the actions of the Tathāgatas, Arhats, Perfectly Enlightened Ones, who alone are

221c

43

ultimate. The actions of arhats and *pratyekabuddha*s are not ultimate. Why? Because phenomena are not inferior, mediocre, or superior, one attains nirvana. Why? With reference to the meaning of the four unconditioned noble truths, the actions of the Tathāgatas, Arhats, Perfectly Enlightened Ones are ultimate. Because all the Tathāgatas, Arhats, Perfectly Enlightened Ones know all future suffering, sever all defilements as well as the sources of all virulent defilements that have been accumulated, and extinguish all the elements in the mind-made bodies [of the three vehicles], they realize the extinction of all suffering.

"O Lord, the extinction of suffering is not the destruction of the Dharma. The 'extinction of suffering' signifies the Dharma body of the Tathāgata, which is from beginningless time uncreated, nonarising, indestructible, free from destruction, eternal, inherently pure, and separate from all the stores of defilement. O Lord, the Dharma body is not separate from, free from, or different from the inconceivable Buddha-Dharmas that are more numerous than the sands of the Ganges River.

"O Lord, the Dharma body of the Tathāgata is called the *tathāgatagarbha* when it is inseparable from the stores of defilement."

Chapter IX

The Underlying Truth:
The Meaning of Emptiness

"O Lord, the wisdom of the *tathāgatagarbha* is the Tathāgata's wisdom of emptiness (*śūnyatā*). O Lord, the *tathāgatagarbha* has not been seen nor attained originally by all the arhats, *pratyeka-buddha*s, and powerful bodhisattvas.

"O Lord, there are two kinds of wisdom of emptiness with reference to the *tathāgatagarbha*. The *tathāgatagarbha* that is empty is separate from, free from, and different from the stores of all defilements. And the *tathāgatagarbha* that is not empty is not separate from, not free from, and not different from the inconceivable Buddha-Dharmas more numerous than the sands of the Ganges River.

"O Lord, the various great disciples can believe in the Tathā-gata with reference to the two wisdoms of emptiness. All arhats and *pratyekabuddha*s revolve in the realm of the four contrary views because of their knowledge of emptiness. Thus, arhats and *pratyekabuddha*s do not originally see nor attain [the wisdom of the *tathāgatagarbha*]. The extinction of all suffering is only realized by the Buddhas who destroy the stores of all defilements and practice the path that extinguishes all suffering."

Chapter X

The One Noble Truth

"O Lord, among these four noble truths, three are impermanent and one is permanent. Why? Because three of the [four] noble truths are conditioned. What is 'conditioned' is impermanent and what is 'impermanent' is false and deceptive in nature. What is 'false and deceptive in nature' is not true, is impermanent, and is not a refuge. Therefore, the [three] noble truths, namely, 'there is suffering,' 'there is the source of suffering,' and 'there is the path,' are not the supreme truth for they are neither permanent nor a refuge."

Chapter XI

The One Refuge

"The one noble truth, namely, 'the extinction of suffering,' is sep-222a arate from the conditioned. What is 'separate from the conditioned' is permanent. What is 'permanent' is not false and deceptive in nature. What is 'not false and deceptive in nature' is true, permanent, and a refuge. Therefore, the noble truth of the extinction [of suffering] is the supreme truth."

Chapter XII

The Contrary Truths

"The noble truth of the extinction [of suffering] is inconceivable, transcending all the conditions of the consciousness of living beings. This is also not the knowledge of arhats and *pratyekabuddhas* who, like those born blind, cannot see all shapes; or like a week-old infant who cannot see the disc of the moon. The truth of the extinction of suffering, similarly, does not belong to the condition of the common person's consciousness nor to the two vehicles' realm of knowledge. The common person's consciousness refers to the two contrary views. The wisdom of all arhats and *pratyekabuddhas* is pure [in comparison with that of the common person].

"'Limited views' refer to the common person's adherence to the misconception that there is a substantial ego within the five psychophysical elements (*skandhas*), which then causes the two views that are designated 'contrary,' namely, eternalism and nihilism. If one considers the conditioned states impermanent, this is nihilism and not the correct view. If one considers nirvana permanent, this is eternalism and not the correct view. Because of misconceptions, there are such views.

"In the sense organs of the body, which are discriminative in nature, some perceive the destruction of phenomena in the present moment. Unable to see phenomena in continuity, they become nihilistic in their views because of misconceptions. The ignorant, who are unable to uderstand or know the momentary consciousness with reference to its continuity, become eternalistic in their views because of misconceptions. By this or that principle, they discriminate and maintain inadequate positions to an extreme degree. Because of foolish misconceptions they adhere to erroneous conceptions and contrary views, namely, nihilism and eternalism.

"O Lord, living beings have contrary ideas when they have acquired the five psychophysical elements of the individual. The impermanent is considered permanent, suffering is considered happiness. The nonsubstantiality of the self is considered a substantial self, the impure is considered pure. The knowledge of all arhats and *pratyekabuddhas* has not originally apprehended the Dharma body of the Tathāgata nor the realm of his omniscience. If there are living beings who believe in the Buddha's words, they will have thoughts of permanence, of happiness, of self, and of purity. These are not contrary views but are correct views. Why? The Dharma body of the Tathāgata is the perfection of permanence, the perfection of happiness, the perfection of the substantial self, and the perfection of purity. Those who see the Dharma body of the Buddha in this way are said to see correctly. Those who see correctly are the true sons and daughters of the Buddha. They arise from the Buddha's words, from the True Dharma, and from conversion to the Dharma, attaining the remaining benefits of the Dharma.

"O Lord, pure wisdom is the perfection of wisdom that belongs to all arhats and *pratyekabuddhas*. This pure wisdom, although it is called pure wisdom, with reference to the [conditioned noble] truth of the extinction [of suffering] is not the realm [of unconditioned wisdom]. Of course, the wisdom of [those beginning to study] the four basic truths (i.e., the four noble truths) also [does not belong to the realm of unconditioned wisdom]. Why? The three vehicles' first actions were not ignorant of the Dharma. Because of their principles, they understood and attained [enlightenment]. The Buddha explained the four basic truths for their sake. O Lord, these four basic truths are the Dharma of the world. O Lord, the one refuge is all refuges. It is the transcendental and supreme refuge, namely, the truth of the extinction [of suffering]."

222b

Chapter XIII

The Inherently Pure

"O Lord, the cycle of birth and death depends on the *tathāgata-garbha,* because the *tathāgatagarbha* is referred to as the original limit [of the cycle of birth and death], which is unknowable. O Lord, *'tathāgatagarbha'* is referred to as the cycle of birth and death for a proper designation. O Lord, the cycle of birth and death is the extinction of the senses and the subsequent arising of [new] inexperienced senses. This is called the cycle of birth and death.

"O Lord, these two phenomena—birth and death—are the *tathāgatagarbha.* It is worldly convention to say 'there is birth' and 'there is death.' 'Death' is the extinction of one's senses. 'Birth' is the arising of new senses.

"The *tathāgatagarbha* is neither life nor death. The *tathāgata-garbha* is separate from the conditioned. The *tathāgatagarbha* is eternal and unchanging. Therefore, the *tathāgatagarbha* is the basis, the support, and the foundation. O Lord, the *tathāgata-garbha* is not separate, not severed, not liberated from, and not different from the inconceivable Buddha-Dharmas. O Lord, the basis, support, and foundation of conditioned phenomena, which are severed from, separate from, and different from the Buddha-Dharmas, [also] are the *tathāgatagarbha.*

"O Lord, if there were no *tathāgatagarbha* there would be no revulsion toward suffering, nor aspiration to seek nirvana. Why? Because the seven [mental] phenomena—the six [sense] consciousnesses and the knowledge of [their accompanying] mental phenomena—do not continue even momentarily and do not accept the impressions of suffering, there cannot be revulsion for suffering nor aspiration to seek nirvana.

"The *tathāgatagarbha* is without any prior limit, is nonarising, and is indestructible, accepting suffering, having revulsion toward suffering, and aspiring to nirvana. O Lord, the *tathāgatagarbha* is not a substantial self, nor a living being, nor 'fate,' nor a person. The *tathāgatagarbha* is not a realm for living beings who have degenerated into the belief of a substantially existent body or for those who have contrary views, or who have minds bewildered by emptiness.

"O Lord, the *tathāgatagarbha* is the womb of the *dharma*s, the womb of the Dharma body, the transcendental womb, and the inherently pure womb. This *tathāgatagarbha* that is inherently pure is the inconceivable realm of the Tathāgata that has been contaminated by extrinsic defilements and other virulent defilements. Why? The good mind is momentary and not contaminated by defilements. The evil mind is also momentary but is not contaminated by defilements either. Defilements do not affect the mind. The mind does not affect defilements. Then how does the mind, which is unaffected by nature, become defiled? O Lord, there are defilements and there are defiled minds. The fact that there is defilement in a mind that is inherently pure is difficult to comprehend. Only the Buddhas, the Lords, who have the eye of truth and the wisdom of truth, who are the sources of the Dharma and penetrate the Dharma, and who are the refuge of the True Dharma, can comprehend this truth."

222c

When Queen Śrīmālā had explained the difficulties in comprehending [the inherently pure mind's defilement], she was questioned by the Buddha. The Buddha, with extreme joy, praised her, "Yes, it is so! It is so! The fact that there is defilement in a mind that is inherently pure is difficult to comprehend. There are two subjects that are difficult to completely comprehend. They are the mind that is inherently pure and the fact that this [same] mind has been contaminated by defilements. These two subjects can be heard by you and the bodhisattva *mahāsattva*s who have the great Dharma. The others, namely, the disciples, can only believe through the Buddha's words."

54

Chapter XIV

The True Sons [and Daughters] of the Tathāgata

[The Buddha said,] "If my disciples comply with their [early stages of] faith and [subsequent] more fervent faith, then they will attain the ultimate after completing their subsequent wisdom of the Dharma that is based upon the illumination of faith. 'The subsequent wisdom of the Dharma' is the insight and fundamental investigation into the realms of sensation and consciousness; insight into karmic retribution; insight into the eye of the arhat; insight into the happiness of the autonomy of mind and into the happiness of meditation; and insight into the supernatural powers of the arhats, *pratyekabuddhas*, and powerful bodhisattvas. When these five kinds of insight have been completed, even after my final nirvana, in future generations, my disciples who have [the early stages of] faith, the [subsequent] more fervent faith, and the subsequent wisdom of the Dharma that is based upon the illumination of faith will attain the ultimate even though their inherently pure minds become contaminated by defilements. The 'ultimate' is the cause for entering the path of the Mahayana. Faith in the Tathāgata has great benefits. Do not slander my [Dharma's] profound meaning."

Then Queen Śrīmālā said to the Buddha, "There are still remaining great benefits which I will explain, with the Buddha's permission."

The Buddha said, "Again, please explain."

Queen Śrīmālā said to the Buddha, "The three kinds of good sons and daughters who, within the most profound meaning [of the Dharma], have separated themselves from injury [to the

55

Dharma], produce great merits, entering the path of the Mahayana. What are the three [kinds of good sons and daughters]? They are those good sons and daughters who 1) develop their own wisdom of the most profound Dharma, 2) develop the subsequent wisdom of the Dharma [that is based upon the illumination of faith], and 3) revere the Lord though they do not completely understand the most profound Dharma.

"What is known only by the Buddhas is not our realm. These [above-mentioned] are called the good sons and daughters who revere the Tathāgata. Only these are the good sons and daughters."

Chapter XV

Śrīmālā

[Śrīmālā said,] "All the remaining living beings who stubbornly cling to false teachings, instead of to the most profound Dharma, turn their backs to the True Dharma and habitually practice the corrupt ways of various heterodoxies. These corrupt ways must be subdued by the [Dharma] King's powers and by the powers of the divine *nāga*s."

When Queen Śrīmālā and her attendants paid obeisance to the Buddha, the Buddha said, "Excellent, excellent, Queen Śrīmālā! In the most profound Dharma, protected by skillful means, subdue what is not the Dharma. Maintain well its correctness. You have already been very close to the hundreds of millions of Buddhas and can explain this [Dharma's] meaning."

At that time the Lord emitted a most excellent light, radiating everywhere over the assembly. His body ascended into the sky, higher than seven *tala* trees. Walking in the sky, he returned to the kingdom of Śrāvastī. Then Queen Śrīmālā and her attendants together faced the Buddha and were transfixed by the sight of him, not moving for even a moment. [The Buddha,] having passed through their field of vision, caused them to be exalted. Each individual praised the Tathāgata's merits and was mindful of him. The Buddha then reentered the city. Turning toward [her husband,] King Mitrayaśas, Queen Śrīmālā praised the Mahayana. All the women of the city, seven years of age and older, were converted to the Mahayana. King Mitrayaśas was also converted to the Mahayana. All the men, seven years of age and older, were converted to the Mahayana. Then all the citizens of the state were turned toward the Mahayana.

Then the Lord entered the Jeta Garden, spoke to the venerable Ānanda, and called upon Śakra, the king of heaven. Śakra, along with his retinue, immediately arrived in the presence of the Buddha. Then the Lord turned toward the king of heaven, Śakra, and to the venerable Ānanda and extensively explained this text. Having explained it, he said to Lord Śakra, "You should accept and read this sutra, O Kauśika. Good sons and daughters, in innumerable *kalpa*s as numerous as the sands of the Ganges River, cultivate the practice of enlightenment and practice the six perfections. If these good sons and daughters learn and read this sutra and uphold it, their blessings will be immense.

"How much more [advantageous] will it be for those who explain this text. Thus, O Kauśika, you must read this sutra on behalf of the thirty-three heavens, defining and extensively explaining it."

Then the Buddha said to Ānanda, "You also must accept and read this sutra. For the sake of the four groups of followers you must extensively explain this sutra."

Then the king of heaven, Śakra, asked the Buddha, "O Lord, what is the name of this sutra? How does one adhere [to its teaching]?"

The Buddha said to Lord Śakra, "This sutra has immeasurable and limitless merits. All the disciples and Buddhas cannot, ultimately, have insight into [these merits] nor know them. Kauśika, you should know all the great merits that are so subtle and profound in this sutra. Now I shall, on your behalf, briefly explain its name. Listen well, listen well and remember this [text]."

Then the king of heaven, Śakra, and the venerable Ānanda said to the Buddha, "Excellent, O Lord! Yes, we will do as you have instructed."

The Buddha said, "This sutra praises the supreme merits of the True Dharma of the Tathāgata [in Chapter I]. In this manner accept it. It explains [in Chapter II] the ten inconceivable ordination vows. In this manner accept it. It explains [in Chapter III] the great aspiration that embraces all aspirations. In this manner

223b

58

accept it. It explains [in Chapter IV] the inconceivable acceptance of the True Dharma. In this manner accept it. It explains [in Chapter V] the entrance into the One Vehicle. In this manner accept it. It explains [in Chapter VI] the unlimited noble truths. In this manner accept it. It explains [in Chapter VII] the *tathāgatagarbha*. In this manner accept it. It explains [in Chapter VIII] the Dharma body. In this manner accept it. It explains [in Chapter IX] the underlying truth: the meaning of emptiness. In this manner accept it. It explains [in Chapter X] the one [noble] truth. In this manner accept it. It explains [in Chapter XI] the one refuge that is eternal and quiescent. In this manner accept it. It explains [in Chapter XII] the contrary truths. In this manner accept it. It explains [in Chapter XIII] the inherently pure mind that is covered [by defilements]. In this manner accept it. It explains [in Chapter XIV] the true sons [and daughters] of the Tathāgata. In this manner accept it. Teach the *Sutra of Queen Śrīmālā of the Lion's Roar*. In this manner accept it.

"Again, O Kauśika, the explanations of this sutra eliminate all doubts. Be steadfast in the complete meaning [of this text] and enter the path of the One Vehicle. O Kauśika, today this scripture, the *Sutra of Queen Śrīmālā of the Lion's Roar,* has been transmitted to you. As long as the Dharma continues, accept, read, extensively define, and explain [this sutra]."

Lord Śakra said to the Buddha, "Very well, O Lord, we will reverently receive your holy teaching." Then the king of heaven, Śakra, the venerable Ānanda, and all the great assemblies of gods, *asura*s, and *gandharva*s, among others, heard the Buddha's teaching and joyfully put it into practice.

End of the Sutra of Queen Śrīmālā of the Lion's Roar

Bibliography

Paul, Diana. "A Prolegomena to the '*Śrīmālādevī Sūtra*' and the *Tathāgata-garbha* Theory: The Role of Women in Buddhism." Dissertation. Madison, WI: University of Wisconsin, 1974.

—. "The Buddhist Feminine Ideal: Queen Śrīmālā and the *Tathāgatagarbha*." Dissertation. Missoula, MT: Scholars Press, 1980.

—. "The Concept of *Tathāgatagarbha* in the *Śrīmālādevī Sūtra* (*Sheng-man ching*)," *Journal of the American Oriental Society* 99/2 (1979): 191–203.

Takasaki, Jikido. *A Study of the Ratnagotravibhāga (Uttaratantra): Being a Treatise on the Tathāgatagarbha Theory of Mahāyāna Buddhism.* Serie Orientale Roma 33. Rome: Instituto Italiano per il Medio ed Estremo Oriente, 1966.

Wayman, Alex, and Hideko Wayman. *The Lion's Roar of Queen Śrīmālā: A Buddhist Scripture on the Tathāgatagarbha Theory.* New York and London: Columbia University Press, 1974.

Zimmermann, Michael. *A Buddha Within: The Tathāgatagarbhasūtra: The Earliest Exposition of the Buddha-Nature Teaching in India.* Tokyo: International Research Institute for Advanced Buddhology, Soka University, 2002.

THE VIMALAKĪRTI SUTRA

Contents

Translator's Introduction

The *Vimalakīrti Sutra* (*Vimalakīrtinirdeśa-sūtra*) is renowned in contemporary world Buddhism for its breathtaking exposition of the Mahayana doctrine of nonduality, and justifiably so. The text imparts its penetrating insight by first elaborating the manifold nuances of this doctrine in finely honed formal language, next by demonstrating the ideal in exquisite philosophical repartée, and then by dramatizing its lofty understanding in the climax of Vimalakīrti's "thunderous silence." Doctrinally, the *Vimalakīrti Sutra* elaborates ideas deriving from the Perfection of Wisdom (Prajñāpāramitā) literature and stated more formally in the treatises of the Mādhyamika school. Spiritually, the demonstrative quality of Vimalakīrti's silence, and the vivid interactions between him and his interlocutors, imply a deep connection with the later development of the Chinese Chan (Japanese: Zen) school as well.

The intellectual charm of the doctrine of nonduality is only heightened by its being situated in such a spectacular religious world. This is no coldly analytical treatise, no harshly systematic rehearsal of religious dogma, but a lively and inventive depiction of religious dialogue that palpably sparkles with humor, insight — and frequent irruptions of the miraculous. This last quality might be ignored by modernist readers, but its effects are too important to allow the tendency to go unchallenged. A fantastic congregation, including incredible arrays of gods, celestial bodhisattvas, and other beings, is assembled within Vimalakīrti's tiny chamber, where they sit on magnificent thrones of unimaginable size — all without jumbling up against each other, and entirely without contorting the dimensions of the ordinary world. The level of impossibility escalates even more when this congregation is then host to an entirely

67

separate world-system, complete with its own mountains and continents, rivers and oceans, which Vimalakīrti grasps as easily as a potter throwing a lump of clay. And to match this incredible assembly there are miracles aplenty, beginning with heavenly flowers raining from above and instantaneous gender reversals, leading up to the spectacular vision of a galaxy far, far away, where the reigning Buddha teaches by means of fragrance rather than words. To top all of this off, a one-bowl-serves-all take-out meal from that world of fragrance is used to feed—and instruct—Vimalakīrti's guests. (I wonder about the possible efficacy of a chocolate Dharma, but that divine substance is nowhere mentioned!) Though moderate in length the scripture is certainly magnificent in the scale of its vision!

At the heart of it all, of course, is the figure of Vimalakīrti. Throughout the course of the scripture he is identified as a great bodhisattva who formerly lived in the "pure land" of the Buddha Akṣobhya, but who has chosen to be reborn in this world in order to teach the recalcitrant sentient beings here. His current identity as householder is but a pose he has assumed, just as his current illness is but a skillful means he has adopted: both are simply devices by which to teach sentient beings. The householder identity is manifestly impossible: he is celibate but has children, goes to brothels but is chaste, is rich but without desire, etc. The immense improbability of Vimalakīrti's person is undoubtedly part of this religious appeal.

Chinese readers were fascinated with the figure of Vimalakīrti, and it is usually said that he represented a type of religious ideal with which unordained literati could identify. Here was a rich and educated layman who could outperform everyone around him—except, of course, the Buddhas themselves—in every conceivable form of endeavor. He enjoyed every imaginable privilege, yet used his energies solely for the benefit of the community around him, a type of service that resonated with Confucian social ideals. No doubt the popularity of the scripture in East Asia has something to do with this congruence with indigenous social ideals and the fascination Chinese Buddhists and interested intellectuals had in a figure of such diverse and remarkable talents. We should not overlook the active role local clienteles played in determining the selection of Buddhist texts that were presented for them in Chinese translation—the residents of East Asia were not passive recipients of Buddhist missionary activity, but very proactive consumers.

In contrast to the relative obscurity of this text in India and Tibet, where there is no record of even a single commentary nor even of any art historical imagery based on it, from at least the third century of the common era the *Vimalakīrti Sutra* became one of the favorites of the East Asian tradition. There are over fifteen hundred depictions of Vimalakīrti and Mañjuśrī in dialogue known from East Asian painting and sculpture traditions, as well as a series of influential commentaries, and innumerable occasional references to the text and its ideas in both religious and secular writings. This is but one example of the manner in which East Asian Buddhism draws on the universalistic themes developed in the Indian homeland of the religion, even as the overall configurations of the Mahayana in South and East Asia are so profoundly different.

It would be wrong, though, to exaggerate the importance of the *Vimalakīrti Sutra* in China, Korea, or Japan. Although it seems to have been used continuously throughout the East Asian Buddhist tradition, both temporally and geographically, there are obvious limitations in the manner of its use. First, even though the text—like many other Mahayana Buddhist scriptures—recommends its own recitation, there is precious little evidence that it was ever very popular as a devotional text, one to be recited for religious benefit. The *Lotus Sutra (Saddharmapuṇḍarīka-sūtra)* and the Pure Land sutras (*Sukhāvatīvyūha-sūtra, Amitāyurdhyāna-sūtra*) are good examples of sutras used in this manner, of course, and even the massive *Flower Garland Sutra (Buddhāvataṃsaka-sūtra)* was used in the same way. Second, the *Vimalakīrti Sutra* never became the basis for a doctrinal tradition of its own, unlike the other scriptures just mentioned, which were used as scriptural bases of the Tiantai (Korean: Ch'ŏnt'ae; Japanese: Tendai), Pure Land, and Huayan (Hwaŏm; Kegon) schools. It is not merely that no independent "Vimalakīrti school" ever developed; the text is frequently mentioned as one of a number of important

Mahayana texts but it tends to be listed in the middle of the pack, as it were. It was used occasionally for healing purposes in medieval China and Japan, though not as often as other scriptures.

No matter what the time period, readers (both those who read for content and those who recite for religious value) tend to perceive their texts in idiosyncratic ways. One wonders if the medieval Chinese really noticed, for example, that the goal of all of Vimalakīrti's efforts was not to create other enlightened laypeople like himself but to inspire his listeners to become monastics and embark on the bodhisattva path. Although accomplished bodhisattvas might choose to be reborn as laypeople, or as beings of virtually any identity, the text indicates on numerous occasions that the best response to hearing and understanding its doctrine of inconceivable liberation was to leave home to become a monk and undertake training in the grandiose vocation of the bodhisattva. Vimalakīrti's job description, in fact, even included the inspiration of some of his following to dedicate themselves to the goal of achieving "Hinayana" enlightenment. Although the Mahayana goal of *anuttarā samyaksaṃbodhi* (complete, perfect enlightenment) was clearly the highest religious ideal presented, for beings of lesser capacity to select lesser targets was not a failing but an appropriate collateral benefit. Not only does the *Vimalakīrti Sutra* not share in the "One Vehicle" teaching of the *Lotus Sutra,* in which all Buddhist practitioners are destined for perfect Buddhahood, there is also no explicit hint of any recommendation that one should dedicate lifetimes of training to achieving the status of an enlightened layperson.

Modern readers are very interested in the scene in which a goddess upstages the stodgy *śrāvaka* or "Hinayana" monk Śāriputra. In a dramatization of the Vimalakīrti story that I saw in San Francisco in the summer of 2000, in which life-size puppets were used to represent the dramatis personae, the highlight of the performance came when the goddess transforms the bodies of herself and Śāriputra into their contrasting genders (depicted by a quick change of the puppets' heads!). From our perspective, this is an important statement of a traditional Buddhist attitude on the status of women, and thus a meaningful religious statement. However, although I have only begun to browse through the Chinese commentarial literature on the *Vimalakīrti Sutra,* it seems that medieval Chinese interest in this scene was rather different from ours. Whereas for modern people this is primarily a statement about gender, for medieval Chinese (and, I suspect, other East Asian) readers it was primarily a statement about emptiness.

Translating the *Vimalakīrti Sutra* has been a joy, in no small part because of the inherent interest of the text itself, including not only its specific doctrinal formulations but just as importantly its dramatic flair and sense of humor. As well, though, the immense pleasure of preparing this English rendition comes through the great resources that are now available.

The present translation is an English rendition of the Chinese translation by Kumārajīva (350–409 or 413), or rather by the team of Kumārajīva, which included such famously gifted students as Sengzhao (373–414) and Daosheng (360?–434). My goal has indeed been to "represent" the Kumārajīva version of the *Vimalakīrti Sutra,* to create an English version that provides access to the text as it might have been understood by fifth-century Chinese readers. One implication of this decision is that I have rendered the terminology as it occurs in Chinese, without attempting to represent what may have been the underlying Indic (either Sanskrit or Prakrit) terminology, except of course where Chinese characters are used to transliterate the Indic sounds. For example, where *kleśa* might better be rendered "defilement," the Chinese equivalent of *fannao* is given here as "afflictions," because that is what the characters mean. And where the fourth *skandha, saṃskāra,* is best rendered "conditioning forces" or "impulses" based on the Sanskrit, the Chinese counterpart *xing* is given as "processes."

Although I obviously do not have direct access to the mind of medieval Chinese readers, I have made frequent use of the *Zhu Weimojie jing (Taishō Shinshū Daizōkyō* Vol. 38, No. 1775, 327a–420a), the joint commentary to the *Vimalakīrti Sutra* left by Kumārajīva, Sengzhao, and Daosheng, and I have tried to render the sutra in the way that it was understood by these primary figures of the translation team. To be able to consult this commentary, which assembles the comments of the chief translator and his primary assistants in the very translation project involved, was for me a remarkable experience.

Practically speaking, I was unable to consult the joint commentary for every line, but I did check its contents when the Chinese phrasing of the sutra itself seemed questionable in some way. Only rarely if at all did the commentators answer my questions directly, and sometimes (especially toward the end of the text, when the density of their comments decreases) they offered no clue whatsoever. However, in a refreshingly large number of cases some feature of their remarks allowed me to make a choice between reasonable alternatives, to create a suitable English analog to their understanding. I have also frequently consulted the two other extant Chinese translations of the *Vimalakīrti Sutra,* the first (Taishō No. 474) by Zhi Qian (fl. 220–252); and the other (Taishō No. 476) by the famous seventh-century pilgrim Xuanzang (596?–664); on rare occasions I have also consulted the commentary on this later translation by Xuanzang's disciple Ji (often referred to as Kuiji, 632–682), the *Shuo Wuguocheng jingshu* (Taishō No. 1782). In the terms used within the sutra itself, I have frequently sighed in exclamation at the unprecedented quality of this arrangement.

Another aspect of how enjoyable this translation project was is the fact that all the extant relevant Chinese texts are now available in well-proofed electronic versions. As a result, my standard practice has been to type the English translation into a word processing file on the computer screen, alongside text editor windows containing the Zhi Qian, Kumārajīva, and Xuanzang translations and the joint commentary of Kumārajīva, Sengzhao, and Daosheng. A simple search utility has allowed me to look for parallel usages in other Buddhist canonical sources when desired. This is the first time I have been able to do translation work in such a manner, and I must express my profound gratitude to the Chinese Buddhist Electronic Text Association (CBETA, www.cbeta.org) for making this possible.

The *Vimalakīrti Sutra* has already been published four times in English translation, and I made some use of these resources in preparing the present English text. Of these four versions, only two are of the Kumārajīva text, and unfortunately neither is of sufficient quality to justify its extensive use here. Charles Luk's older rendering is too freely interpretive to be of help, and in addition he frequently becomes confused regarding the grammatical construction of the original. Burton Watson's recent translation is better grammatically but his intentional lack of attention to Buddhist technical terms undermines his effort, eliminating a great deal of its intrinsic religious interest. Robert Thurman's translation of the Tibetan version of the *Vimalakīrti Sutra* is a very creditable rendition of that text but there are enough differences between it and Kumārajīva's Chinese version to make extensive use inappropriate here. I have therefore relied primarily on Étienne Lamotte's translation from the Tibetan, even though it sometimes regularizes the text (i.e., adverts to standard Indian Buddhist usages) in ways that the Thurman rendition does not. To be precise, I have used the English translation of Lamotte's work done by Sara Boin (London: Pali Text Society, 1976), which sometimes renders scriptural passages more in line with Lamotte's reconstructed Sanskrit than his translation of the Tibetan. (The preceding characterizations are based in part on Jan Nattier's *"The Teaching of Vimalakīrti* [*Vimalakīrtinirdeśa*]: A Review of Four English Translations," *Buddhist Literature* 2 [2000]: 234–58.) For understanding the Chinese grammar of the Kumārajīva version I have consulted the *"Yuima-gyō,"* a useful modern Japanese translation by Jikidō Takasaki, in his and Kōshō Kawamura's *Yuima-gyō, Shiyaku Bonten shomon kyō, Shuryōgon zammai kyō* [*Vimalakīrti Sūtra, Questions of the Brahmā (Deva) Viśeṣacinti Sūtra, and Śūraṃgama-samādhi Sūtra*], *Monju kyōten* [*Mañjuśrī Scriptures*] no. 2 (Tokyo: Daizō shuppan, 1993), in spite of its emphasis on readings drawn from Lamotte and the Tibetan translation. Recently, a Sanskrit manuscript of the *Vimalakīrti Sutra* has been discovered, and I have acquired transcriptions of selected passages through the kind assistance of Yoshiyasu Yonezawa of Taishō University.

Chapter numbers and titles are as in the Taishō edition; section numbers imitate those in Lamotte, varying only where Kumārajīva's text differs from the Tibetan version followed by Lamotte.

THE SUTRA PREACHED BY VIMALAKĪRTI

Also called "The Inconceivable Emancipation"

Translated by
Tripiṭaka Master Kumārajīva
of the Yao Qin [Dynasty]

Fascicle One

Chapter I

Buddha Land

1. Thus have I heard. At one time the Buddha was in the garden 537a7 of Āmrapālī near Vaiśālī, in the company of a great congregation of eight thousand *bhikṣu*s.

2. There were thirty-two thousand bodhisattvas, recognized by the congregation.

3. The [bodhisattvas present] had all accomplished the original practices of great wisdom; were established by the numinous charisma of the Buddhas; maintained the correct Dharma for the defense of the Dharma city; made their names heard throughout the ten directions through their ability at the lion's roar; befriended and pacified people without being requested; exalted the Three Jewels (Buddha, Dharma, and Sangha) and were thus able to keep them from being cut off; subjugated the vengeful Māras and controlled those of the heterodox paths; were entirely purified and had forever transcended the impediments (i.e., afflictions); maintained their minds always in peace and unhindered emancipation; were unfailing in their mindfulness, concentration, *dhāraṇī* (i.e., memorization of the Dharma), and eloquence; were replete in charity (*dāna*), morality (*śīla*), forbearance (*kṣānti*), exertion (*vīrya*), meditation (*dhyāna*), wisdom (*prajñā*), and the power of skillful means; had attained the forbearance of the nonarising of *dharma*s and the nonattainment [of all things]; were able to accord with [the truth] in turning the irreversible wheel [of the Dharma];

77

understood well the characteristics of the *dharma*s and understood the capacities (lit., "roots") of sentient beings; had attained fearlessness in sheltering the great congregations; cultivated their minds with merit and wisdom; were paramount in the adornment of their bodies with the [thirty-two primary] characteristics and [eighty subsidiary] marks; had dispensed with worldly adornments; were known above and beyond even Mount Sumeru; were firmly resolute in faith like *vajra* (i.e., diamond); illuminated the Dharma jewel everywhere and rained down the sweet dew [of the Dharma]; were paramount in the subtleties of the host of [spoken] sounds; profoundly entered into conditioned generation to eliminate the false views; were without any residual influence of the two extremes of being and nonbeing; preached the Dharma without fear like the lion's roar; preached with reverberations like thunder; were without measure and beyond measurement; were like ocean captains who had collected the many Dharma jewels; comprehended the profound and wondrous meanings of the Dharmas; understood well the past tendencies and [current] mental processes of sentient beings; approached the unparalleled autonomous wisdom of the Buddha, the ten powers, [the four] fearlessnesses, and all the eighteen exclusive [attributes of the Buddha]; had closed all the doorways of the evil destinations but were born in the five destinations in order to manifest their bodies there; were great medicine kings who were good at healing the various illnesses; provided medicine according to the illness and caused it to be taken; were accomplished in all the immeasurable merits; had ornamented and purified all the imeasurable Buddha lands; unfailingly used what they saw and heard for the benefit [of others]; and never squandered away their endeavors. Thus were they entirely replete in all merits.

537b

4. Their names were Equivalent Contemplation Bodhisattva, Inequivalent Contemplation Bodhisattva, Equivalent-Inequivalent Contemplation Bodhisattva, Autonomy of Meditation King Bodhisattva, Autonomous Dharma King Bodhisattva, Dharma Characteristic Bodhisattva, Radiance Characteristic Bodhisattva, Radiance Ornament Bodhisattva, Great Ornament Bodhisattva,

Accumulation of Jewels Bodhisattva, Accumulation of Eloquence
Bodhisattva, Jewel Hand Bodhisattva, Jewel Seal Hand Bodhisattva, Constantly Raised Hand Bodhisattva, Constantly Lowered
Hand Bodhisattva, Constantly Lamenting Bodhisattva, Roots of
Joy Bodhisattva, Joy King Bodhisattva, Eloquent Sound Bodhi-
sattva, Store of Space Bodhisattva, Holding the Jewel Torch Bodhi-
sattva, Jewel Courage Bodhisattva, Jewel Vision Bodhisattva,
Indra's Net Bodhisattva, Illumination Net Bodhisattva, Uncondi-
tional Contemplation Bodhisattva, Accumulation of Wisdom Bodhi-
sattva, Excellent Jewel Bodhisattva, Heavenly King Bodhisattva,
Destroyer of Māra Bodhisattva, Lightning-like Virtue Bodhisattva,
Autonomous King Bodhisattva, Ornament of the Characteristics
of Merit Bodhisattva, Lion's Roar Bodhisattva, Sound of Thunder
Bodhisattva, Sound Striking the Mountains Bodhisattva, Fragrant
Elephant Bodhisattva, White Fragrant Elephant Bodhisattva,
Constant Exertion Bodhisattva, Unresting Bodhisattva, Wondrous
Birth Bodhisattva, Flower Ornament Bodhisattva, Contemplates
the Sounds of the World (Avalokiteśvara) Bodhisattva, Attains
Great Strength Bodhisattva, Brahmā's Net Bodhisattva, Jewel
Staff Bodhisattva, Undefeated Bodhisattva, Ornamented Earth
Bodhisattva, Golden Crest Bodhisattva, Pearl Crest Bodhisattva,
Maitreya Bodhisattva, Mañjuśrī Dharma Prince Bodhisattva—
there were thirty-two thousand such as these.

5. There were also ten thousand Brahmā heavenly kings,
Śikhin and others, who descended from the other worlds of four
continents to proceed to where the Buddha was in order to hear
the Dharma. There were also twelve thousand heavenly emper-
ors (i.e., Indras), who also came from the other worlds of four continents to sit in this assembly, and the other awesomely powerful
gods (*devas*), dragons (*nāgas*), *yakṣas*, *gandharvas*, *asuras*, *garuḍas*,
kiṃnaras, and *mahoragas*, who all came to sit in the assembly.
The *bhikṣus* (monks), *bhikṣuṇīs* (nuns), *upāsakas* (laymen), and
upāsikās (laywomen) [also] came together to sit in the assembly.

6. At that time the Buddha explained the Dharma for the congregation of immeasurable hundreds of thousands surrounding and

revering him. He was like [Mount] Sumeru, the king of mountains, rising high above the ocean. Peacefully seated on the many-jeweled lion seat, he towered over the great congregation of all those who had come there.

7. At that time there was an elder's son in the city of Vaiśālī named Jewel Accumulation. He and five hundred other elders' sons proceeded to where the Buddha was, holding canopies made of the seven treasures. Reverencing [the Buddha's] feet with their heads, they all simultaneously offered their canopies to the Buddha.

8. The Buddha's numinous charisma made the jewel-laden canopies all turn into a single canopy, which covered the entire trimegachiliocosm, yet allowing all the characteristics of the breadth and length of this world to appear within it. Also, all the trimegachiliocosm's Mount Sumerus, Snowy Mountains, Mucilinda Mountains, Mahāmucilinda Mountains, Fragrant Mountains, Jewel Mountains, Golden Mountains, Black Mountains, Iron Ring Mountains, and Great Iron Ring Mountains; the oceans, rivers, streams, and springs; the suns, moons, and stars; the palaces of the gods, the palaces of the dragons, and the palaces of the honored gods— all these appeared within that jewel-laden canopy. Also, the Buddhas of the ten directions, as well as the Buddhas' preaching of the Dharma, also appeared in that jewel-laden canopy.

537c

9. At that time the entire great congregation observed the numinous power of the Buddha and exclaimed in praise of its unprecedented [quality]. They held their palms together and reverenced the Buddha, gazing up at his revered countenance without interruption.

10. At this the elder's son Jewel Accumulation proclaimed in verse before the Buddha:

1. Your eyes are pure,
   And as large as blue lotuses;
   Your mind is pure, having mastered the concentrations.
   Long have you accumulated pure action—you are
      immeasurably praiseworthy;

You have guided the congregation with serenity, and
therefore we bow our heads to you.

2. We see the Great Sage use numinous transformations
To manifest the immeasurable lands throughout the ten
directions,
Within which the Buddhas preach the Dharma,
And we thus can see and hear them all!

3. The Dharma power of the Dharma King surpasses all
other beings,
And you always give the wealth of Dharma to all.
Well do you discriminate the characteristics of the *dhar-
ma*s and remain unmoved within the cardinal principle.
You have already achieved autonomy with regard to the
*dharma*s, and therefore we bow our heads to you as
Dharma King.

4. You explain that the *dharma*s are neither extant nor
non-extant,
Although the *dharma*s are generated from causes and
conditions;
That they are without self, without creation, without
experiencer,
Although good and evil karma is also not extinguished.

5. Initially, under the *bodhi* tree you forcefully subjugated
Māra,
Attaining extinction, like sweet dew, and achieving
enlightenment.
Without any intention in mind and without
experiencing any process,
You thoroughly vanquished the heterodox paths.

6. With three turnings of the wheel of the Dharma in the
chiliocosm,
The wheel is fundamentally always pure.

The achievement of enlightenment by gods and humans
   attests to this,
And the Three Jewels are thus manifest in the world.

7. With this wondrous Dharma you save sentient beings,
   Who after experiencing it never regress from permanent
      serenity.
   As the Great Medicine King who saves us from old age,
      illness, and death,
   You should be worshiped as a Dharma sea whose virtues
      are boundless.

8. Immovable before abuse and praise, like [Mount] Sumeru,
   You are equally compassionate to those who are good
      or not.
   Your mental processes are universally same, like
      space—
   Who could hear of the Jewel Among Humans without
      becoming devoted [to you]?

9. Now we offer the World-honored One this subtle canopy
   Within which is manifested to us the trimegachiliocosm,
   Including the palaces in which the gods and dragons
      abide,
   As well as the *gandharvas* and *yakṣas*.

10. We see all that transpires in the world,
   As He of the Ten Powers compassionately manifests
      these transformations.
   The congregation has observed this rare event and all
      exclaimed in praise of the Buddha,
   And now we bow our heads to the Honored One of the
      triple world.

11. [You,] the Great Sage and Dharma King, are the refuge
      of the congregation,
   Who purify their minds in contemplating [you,] the
      Buddha, all of them in ecstasy.

538a

They each see the World-honored One in front of himself,
Through the [eighteen] exclusive attributes of [the
Buddha's] numinous power.

12. The Buddha explains the Dharma with one sound,
And sentient beings each attain understanding
according to their capacity.
Each one says the World-honored One is speaking his
own language,
Through the exclusive attribute of [the Buddha's]
numinous power.

13. The Buddha preaches the Dharma with one sound,
And sentient beings each understand accordingly.
Everyone accepts and practices it, and receives its benefit,
Through the exclusive attribute of [the Buddha's]
numinous power.

14. The Buddha preaches the Dharma with one sound,
But some are afraid and some joyous.
Some generate revulsion [to the world of suffering] or
eliminate their doubts,
Through the exclusive attribute of [the Buddha's]
numinous power.

15. We bow our heads to Him of the Ten Powers and Great
Exertion.
We bow our heads to Him Who Has Achieved
Fearlessness.
We bow our heads to Him Residing in the Exclusive
Attributes.
We bow our heads to the Great Guide of All.

16. We bow our heads to Him Who Can Eradicate the
Fetters.
We bow our heads to Him Who Has Arrived at the
Other Shore.

We bow our heads to Him Who Can Save [Beings in All]
the Worlds.
We bow our heads to Him Who Has Eternally
Transcended the Realm of Samsara.

17. You understand the past and future characteristics of
sentient beings,
And well have you attained emancipation with regard to
the *dharma*s.
Unattached to the world, like the lotus flower [growing
out of the mud],
You always enter well into the practice of empty
serenity (i.e., nirvana).

18. You have attained the characteristics of the *dharma*s
without hindrance,
And we bow our heads to Him Who Relies On Nothing,
Like Space.

11. When the elder's son Jewel Accumulation finished speaking this verse, he addressed the Buddha, "World-honored One, these five hundred elders' sons have all generated the intention to achieve *anuttarā samyaksaṃbodhi* (complete, perfect enlightenment). We wish to hear of the purity of the countries of the Buddha. Would the World-honored One please explain for the bodhisattvas the practices by which a land is purified?"

The Buddha said, "Excellent, Jewel Accumulation! You are able to inquire on behalf of the bodhisattvas regarding the practices by which the Tathāgata purified his land. Listen clearly, listen clearly, and consider this well. I will explain it for you." At this Jewel Accumulation and the five hundred elders' sons listened as instructed.

12. The Buddha said, "Jewel Accumulation, the categories of sentient beings are the bodhisattvas' Buddha lands. Why is this? Bodhisattvas acquire the Buddha lands according to the sentient beings they convert. They acquire the Buddha lands according to the sentient beings they discipline. They acquire the Buddha lands according to what country sentient beings need to enter into

Buddha wisdom. They acquire the Buddha lands according to what country sentient beings need to generate the roots [for becoming] bodhisattvas. Why is this? Because bodhisattvas' acquisition of the pure countries is entirely for the benefit of sentient beings. It is like a man who wants to build a palace on empty land who is [able to build it] according to his wish without hindrance. He would never be able to build it in space. Bodhisattvas are like this. In order to accomplish the [salvation of] sentient beings, they vow to acquire the Buddha countries. The vow to acquire a Buddha land is not done in empty space!

13. "Jewel Accumulation, you should understand that sincer- 538b
ity is the bodhisattva's pure land—when the bodhisattva attains Buddhahood, it is sentient beings who do not flatter [and lie] that come be born in his country.

"A profound mind is the bodhisattva's pure land—when the bodhisattva attains Buddhahood, it is sentient beings who are complete in merit that come to be born in his country.

"The mind of *bodhi* (*bodhicitta,* i.e., the intention to achieve perfect enlightenment) is the bodhisattva's pure land—when the bodhisattva achieves Buddhahood, sentient beings of the Mahayana come to be born in his country.

"Charity (*dāna*) is the bodhisattva's pure land—all sentient beings capable of renunciation come to be born in his country.

"Morality (*śīla,* lit., "maintaining the precepts") is the bodhisattva's pure land—when the bodhisattva achieves Buddhahood, sentient beings who have fulfilled their vows to practice the path of the ten types of good come to be born in his country.

"Forbearance (*kṣānti*) is the bodhisattva's pure land—when the bodhisattva achieves Buddhahood, sentient beings who have ornamented themselves with the thirty-two marks [of a Buddha] come to be born in his country.

"Exertion (*vīrya*) is the bodhisattva's pure land—when the bodhisattva achieves Buddhahood, sentient beings who have energetically cultivated all the [types of] merit come to be born in his country.

"Meditation (*dhyāna*) is the bodhisattva's pure land—when the bodhisattva achieves Buddhahood, sentient beings who control their minds and keep them undisturbed come to be born in his country.

"Wisdom (*prajñā*) is the bodhisattva's pure land—when the bodhisattva achieves Buddhahood, sentient beings who [have achieved] correct concentration come to be born in his country.

"The four unlimited states of mind (i.e., the *brahma-vihāra*s) are the bodhisattva's pure land—when the bodhisattva achieves Buddhahood, sentient beings who have developed sympathy, compassion, joy, and equanimity come to be born in his pure land.

"The four means of attraction are the bodhisattva's pure land—when the bodhisattva achieves Buddhahood, sentient beings who have been attracted through his emancipation come to be born in his country.

"Skillful means are the bodhisattva's pure land—when the bodhisattva achieves Buddhahood, sentient beings whose skillful means are without hindrance regarding all the the *dharma*s come to be born in his country.

"The thirty-seven factors of enlightenment are the bodhisattva's pure land—when the bodhisattva achieves Buddhahood, sentient beings who [have accomplished the] foundations of mindfulness, correct exertions, numinous capabilities, faculties, powers, and the noble path come to be born in his country.

"The attitude of rededication [of merit] is the bodhisattva's pure land—when the bodhisattva achieves Buddhahood, he attains a country that is complete in all [forms of] merit.

"Explaining how to eliminate the eight difficult realms [where the Buddha and Dharma are unknown] is the bodhisattva's pure land—when the bodhisattva achieves Buddhahood, his country is without the three evil destinations and eight difficult realms.

"Maintaining one's own practice of the precepts without reviling the deficiencies of others is the bodhisattva's pure land—when the bodhisattva achieves Buddhahood, his country is without the names (i.e., without even the words) 'violation' and 'prohibition.'

"The ten goods are the bodhisattva's pure land—when the bodhisattva achieves Buddhahood, sentient beings whose lifespans are not interrupted, who are very wealthy, who are chaste, whose words are truthful, who always use gentle language, who do not isolate themselves from their subordinates and who are good at resolving disputes, whose words are always beneficial, who are not jealous, who are not prone to anger, and who have correct views— [all these types of sentient beings] come to be born in his country.

14. "Thus, Jewel Accumulation, according to his sincerity does the bodhisattva generate his practice. According to his generation of practice does he attain the profound mind. According to his profound mind does he discipline his intention. According to the disciplining of his intention does he practice in conformity with the teaching. According to his practice in conformance to the teaching is he able to rededicate [merit].

"According to his rededication does he have skillful means. According to his skillful means does he make sentient beings accomplish [liberation]. According to his accomplishment [of the liberation] of sentient beings is his Buddha land pure. According to the purity of the Buddha land is his explanation of the Dharma pure. According to the purity of his explanation of the Dharma is his wisdom pure. According to the purity of his wisdom is his mind pure. According to the purity of his mind are all his merits pure. 538c

"Therefore, Jewel Accumulation, if a bodhisattva wishes to attain a pure land he should purify his mind. According to the purity of his mind is his Buddha land pure!"

15. At that time Śāriputra was influenced by the Buddha's numinous charisma to have this thought: "If the bodhisattva's Buddha land is pure according to the purity of the bodhisattva's mind, then when our World-honored One was a bodhisattva his mind must have been pure. Nevertheless, this Buddha land is so impure!"

The Buddha knew what he was thinking and asked him, "What do you think? Although the blind do not see them, can the sun and moon be anything but pure?"

[Śāriputra] answered, "No, World-honored One! This is the fault of the blind, not that of the sun and moon."

[The Buddha said], "Śāriputra, it is through the transgressions of sentient beings that they do not see the purity of the Tathāgata's (i.e., my) Buddha land. This is not the Tathāgata's fault! Śāriputra, this land of mine is pure, but you do not see it."

16. At that time Conch Crest Brahmā King said to Śāriputra, "Do not think thus, saying that this Buddha land is not pure. Why? I have witnessed the purity of Śākyamuni's Buddha land. It is like the heavenly palace of Īśvara."

Śāriputra said, "As I observe this land, it is hills and hollows, brambles and gravel, and rocks and mountains—all filled with defilements."

Conch Crest Brahmā King said, "Sir, your mind has (i.e., perceives) high and low because you are not relying on Buddha wisdom. Hence you perceive this land as impure. Śāriputra, the bodhisattva is universally same [in attitude] regarding all sentient beings. The purity of his profound mind relies on Buddha wisdom and therefore is able to perceive the purity of this Buddha land."

17. At this the Buddha pointed to the earth with his toe, and instantly the trimegachiliocosm was as if ornamented with a hundred thousand jewels. It was like the Jewel Ornamentation land, with all its immeasurable merits, of Jewel Ornament Buddha.

The entire great assembly exclaimed at this unprecedented event, and they all saw themselves sitting on many-jeweled lotus flowers.

18. The Buddha told Śāriputra, "You should now observe the purity of this Buddha land."

Śāriputra said, "So it is, World-honored One. Originally I did not see it; originally I did not hear it. Now the purity of the Buddha's country is entirely apparent."

The Buddha said to Śāriputra, "My Buddha country is always pure, like this. It is only so as to save inferior persons here that I manifest it as a defiled and impure land. It is like the many-jeweled eating utensils used in common by the gods, the food in which is of different colors depending on their merits. Just so, Śāriputra, if a person's mind is pure he sees the merits and ornaments of this land."

19. When the Buddha manifested the purity of this country, 539a the five hundred elders' sons led by Jewel Accumulation all achieved forbearance of the nonarising of *dharmas*. Eighty-four thousand people all generated the intention to achieve *anuttarā samyaksaṃbodhi*.

20. The Buddha then withdrew his numinous powers, and the world returned to its former [appearance].

The thirty-two thousand gods and humans who sought the *śrāvaka* vehicle understood that conditioned *dharmas* were all entirely impermanent and, distantly transcending sensory defilement, they attained purity of the Dharma eye.

Eight thousand *bhikṣus* [achieved] nonexperiencing of the *dharmas*, their minds liberated by the elimination of the flaws.

Chapter II

Skillful Means

1. At that time there was within the great city of Vaiśālī an elder named Vimalakīrti. He had already made offerings to immeasurable Buddhas, deeply planting the foundation of goodness. He had attained forbearance of the nonarising [of *dharmas*], and his eloquence was unhindered. He disported in the numinous penetrations and had achieved all the *dhāraṇī*s. He had attained fearlessness and had subjugated the troubling vengeance of the Māras. Entering into [all the] gates of profound Dharma, he was excellent at the perfection of wisdom. Having penetrated skillful means, his great vows had been accomplished. Understanding the tendencies of the minds of sentient beings, he was also able to discriminate between those of sharp and dull faculties. Long [a practitioner of] the path of Buddhahood, his mind was already pure, and he was definitively [dedicated to] the Mahayana. He considered well the activities of the realms of existence, and, residing in the deportment of the Buddha, his mind was great as the ocean. The Buddhas praised him [as their] disciple, and the Indras, Brahmās, and world lords (i.e., heavenly kings) revered him.

2. Wanting to save people, [Vimalakīrti] used his excellent skillful means to reside in Vaiśālī, where with wealth immeasurable he attracted the poor, with the purity of his morality he attracted the miscreants, with the moderation of his forbearance he attracted the angry, with great exertion he attracted the indolent, with singleminded concentration he attracted the perturbed, and with definitive wisdom he attracted the foolish.

3. Although he was a white-robed [layman], he maintained the pure Vinaya conduct of a *śramaṇa;* although he resided in the home, he was not attached to the triple world. He manifested the

91

existence of wife and sons, but always cultivated chastity. He revealed the existence of subordinates, but always enjoyed transcendence. Although his clothing was richly decorated, it was with the marks and features [of a Tathāgata] that he adorned his body. Although he drank and ate, the joy of concentration was his [favorite] flavor. If he went to gambling houses or theaters it was only to save people. He hosted those of the heretic paths without breaking his correct faith. Although he illuminated the profane classics he always took pleasure in the Buddha-Dharma. He was revered by all as the one most worthy of offerings.

4. In supporting the correct Dharma he attracted both old and young. In all of his business dealings, although he made worldly profits he never took joy in them. In wandering the crossroads, he dispensed benefit to sentient beings. In entering into government administration, he safeguarded everyone. In entering into the lecture halls, he led people by means of the Mahayana. In entering the schools, he inspired the children. In entering the brothels, he revealed the transgressions [that arise from] desire. In entering the wine shops, he was able to maintain (lit., "establish") his [good] intention.

5. When he was with the elders, as the most honored of the eminent he explained the excellent Dharma for them. When he was among retired scholars as the most honored of the retired scholars he eradicated their attachments. When he was among *kṣatriyas*, as the most honored among *kṣatriyas* he taught them forbearance. When he was among brahmans, as the most honored among brahmans he eliminated their arrogance. When he was among the ministers, as the most honored among ministers he taught them the correct Dharma.

When he was among princes, as the most honored among princes he instructed them with loyalty and filiality.

When he was among palace officials, as the most honored among palace officials he converted the palace women.

6. When he was among the common people, as the most honored among the common people he had them generate the power of blessings.

539b

When he was among Brahmā gods, as the most honored of the Brahmā gods he taught with superior wisdom.

When he was among Indras, as the most honored among Indras he manifested impermanence.

When he was among world-protector [gods], as the most honored among world-protectors he protected sentient beings.

The Elder Vimalakīrti used immeasurable skillful means such as these to benefit sentient beings.

7. Using skillful means he manifested becoming ill himself. Because he was ill, the king, ministers, elders, retired scholars, brahmans, the princes and the other palace retainers, and innumerable thousands of people all came to inquire about his illness.

8. To those who came, Vimalakīrti used the occasion of his illness to make extensive explanations of the Dharma.

"Sirs, the body is impermanent, without strength, without power, without solidity. Given the way it rapidly disintegrates, it cannot be trusted (i.e., relied upon). Alternately suffering and vexatious, it accumulates a host of illnesses. Sirs, the wise do not rely on such a body.

9. "This body is like a bit of foam that cannot be grasped. This body is like bubbles that do not last very long. This body is like a mirage, generated from thirst. This body is like a banana tree, with nothing solid within. This body is like a phantasm arising from confused [views]. This body is like a dream, an illusory view. This body is like a shadow, manifested through karmic conditions. This body is like an echo, dependent on causes and conditions. This body is like a cloud, which changes and disappears in an instant. This body is like lightning, unstable from one moment to another.

10. "This body is without master, like the earth. This body is without self, like fire. This body is without lifespan, like the wind. This body is without person, like water.

11. "This body is insubstantial, being housed in the four elements. This body is empty, transcending self and the qualities of self. This body is ignorant, like plants and rocks. This body is inactive, being turned by the power of the wind. This body is impure,

replete with defilements. This body is untrustworthy, since even though one washes, clothes, and feeds it it will necessarily disintegrate. This body is a disaster, vexed by a hundred and one illnesses. This body is like a well on a hill, pressed by age. This body is unreliable, dying in spite of being needed. This body is like a poisonous snake, a vengeful bandit, an empty aggregation. It is the composite of the *skandha*s, sensory realms, and sensory capacities.

539c "Sirs, this [body] being so calamitous and repugnant, you should wish for the body of the Buddha. Why?

12. "The body of the Buddha is the body of the Dharma. It is generated through immeasurable wisdom and merit. It is generated through morality, meditation, wisdom, emancipation, and the knowledge and vision of emancipation. It is generated through sympathy, compassion, joy, and equanimity (i.e., the four unlimiteds). It is generated through the perfections of charity, morality, forbearance and adaptability, energetic exertion, meditation, emancipation, *samādhi*, and learned wisdom. It is generated from skillful means; it has been generated from the six penetrations; it is generated from the three illuminations; it is generated from the thirty-seven factors of enlightenment; it has been generated from concentration and contemplation; it is generated from the ten powers, the four fearlessnesses, and the eighteen exclusive attributes; it is generated from the eradication of all the *dharma*s that are not good and accumulation of all the good *dharma*s; it is generated from the truth; it is generated from the absence of negligence.

"The Tathāgata's body is generated from immeasurable pure *dharma*s such as these. Sirs, if you wish to attain the body of the Buddha and eradicate all the illnesses of sentient beings, you should generate the intention to achieve *anuttarā samyaksaṃbodhi*!"

13. Thus did the Elder Vimalakīrti explain the Dharma for those who inquired about his illness, causing innumerable thousands of people to all generate the intention to achieve *anuttarā samyaksaṃbodhi*.

Chapter III

Disciples

1. At that time the Elder Vimalakīrti thought to himself, "I am lying sick in bed. How can the World-honored One, He of Great Sympathy, not take pity on me?"

2. Knowing what [Vimalakīrti] was thinking, the Buddha immediately told Śāriputra, "Go visit Vimalakīrti and inquire about his illness."

Śāriputra addressed the Buddha, "World-honored One, I dare not accept your instruction to go inquire about his illness. Why? I remember once in the past, when I was sitting in repose beneath a tree. At the time Vimalakīrti came and said to me,

3. "'O Śāriputra, you need not take this sitting [in meditation] to be sitting in repose. Sitting in repose is to not manifest body and mind in the triple world—this is sitting in repose. To generate the concentration of extinction while manifesting the deportments— this is sitting in repose. Not to relinquish the Dharma of enlightenment and yet manifest the affairs of [ordinary] sentient beings— this is sitting in repose. To have the mind neither abide internally nor locate itself externally—this is sitting in repose. To be unmoved by the [sixty-two mistaken] views yet cultivate the thirty-seven factors of enlightenment—this is sitting in repose. Not to eradicate the afflictions yet enter into nirvana—this is sitting in repose.

"'Those who are able to sit in this fashion [will receive] the Buddha's seal of approval.'

4. "At the time, World-honored One, I simply listened to this explanation in silence and was unable to respond. Therefore, I cannot accept your instruction to go inquire about his illness."

5. The Buddha told Mahāmaudgalyāyana, "You go inquire about Vimalakīrti's illness."

Maudgalyāyana addressed the Buddha, "World-honored One, I dare not accept your instruction to go inquire about his illness. Why? I remember once in the past, I had entered the great city of Vaiśālī and was explaining the Dharma to the retired scholars of a certain neighborhood. At the time Vimalakīrti came and said to me,

540a

6. "'O Mahāmaudgalyāyana, when you explain the Dharma to white-robed retired scholars, you should not explain it as you are now doing. In explaining the Dharma, you should explain according to the Dharma.

"'The Dharma is without sentient beings because it transcends the defilements of sentient beings; the Dharma is without self because it transcends the defilements of self; the Dharma is without lifespan because it transcends birth and death (samsara); and the Dharma is without person because it eradicates the threshold between previous and subsequent [moments].

"'The Dharma is permanently serene because it extinguishes the characteristics; the Dharma transcends characteristics because it is without conditions; the Dharma is without names because it eradicates words; the Dharma is without explanation because it transcends discursive thought and reasoning; the Dharma is without the characteristics of form because it is like space; the Dharma is without hypotheses because it is ultimately empty; the Dharma is without the sense of personal possession because it transcends personal possession; the Dharma is without discrimination because it transcends the consciousnesses; and the Dharma is incomparable because there is nothing to match it; the Dharma is divorced from causation because it is not located in conditionality.

"'The Dharma is identical to Dharma-nature because it inheres in the *dharmas*; the Dharma accords with suchness because it is without anything that accords with it; the Dharma abides in the actual because it is unmoved by the extremes; the Dharma is motionless because it is not dependent on the six types of sensory data; and the Dharma is without past and future because it is constantly nonabiding.

"'The Dharma concurs with emptiness, accords with the absence of characteristics, and responds to inactivity. The Dharma transcends good and ugly, the Dharma is without gain and loss, the Dharma is without generation and extinction, and the Dharma is without refuge. The Dharma surpasses eye, ear, nose, tongue, body, and mind. The Dharma is without high and low, the Dharma abides constantly without moving, and the Dharma transcends all practices of contemplation.

7. "'O Mahāmaudgalyāyana, with characteristics such as these, how can the Dharma be explained? Explaining the Dharma should be without explaining and without indicating. Listening to the Dharma should be without listening and without attaining.

"'It is like a magician explaining the Dharma to conjured people.

8. "'One should have such a mindset in explaining the Dharma; one should comprehend that the faculties of sentient beings [include both] sharp and dull. You would do well to be without hindrance in your knowledge and vision. Use the mind of great compassion and praise the Mahayana. Remember to recompense the kindness of the Buddha and do not cut off the Three Jewels. Thus should you explain the Dharma.'

9. "When Vimalakīrti explained this Dharma, eight hundred retired scholars generated the intention to achieve *anuttarā samyaksaṃbodhi*. I lack this eloquence. Therefore I cannot accept [your instruction] to go inquire about his illness."

10. The Buddha told Mahākāśyapa, "You go inquire about Vimalakīrti's illness."

Kāśyapa addressed the Buddha, "World-honored One, I dare not accept your instruction to go inquire about his illness. Why? I remember once in the past, when I was begging in a poor neighborhood, Vimalakīrti came and said to me,

11. "'O Mahākāśyapa, you have the mind of sympathy and compassion but are unable [to apply it] universally. You have abandoned the wealthy to beg from the poor.

"'Kāśyapa, while abiding in the Dharma of universal sameness, you should proceed in sequence in your begging.

"'It is because of not eating that you should practice begging.

"'It is because of the destruction of one's physical integrity that you should take that lump of food. It is because of not receiving that you should receive that food.

"'You should enter a village with the idea that it is an empty aggregation.

12. "'The forms you see are equivalent to [what] the blind [see]; the sounds you hear are equivalent to echoes; the fragrances you smell are equivalent to the wind; the flavors you eat should not be discriminated; your tactile sensations are like the realizations of wisdom; and you should understand that the *dharmas* are like phantasms. That which is without self-nature and without other-nature originally was not burning and will not become extinguished now.

13. "'Kāśyapa, if you are able to enter the eight emancipations without renouncing the eight perversions, using the characteristic of perversion to enter into the correct Dharma, and using a single meal to give to all, making offerings to the Buddhas and the assembly of worthies and sages—only then should you eat.

"'To eat in this fashion is neither to have the afflictions nor to transcend the afflictions, it is neither to enter into concentration nor to arise from concentration, it is neither to abide in the world nor to abide in nirvana.

"'Where there is charity, there are neither great nor small blessings, neither benefit nor harm. This is the correct entry into the path of Buddhahood, without relying on the *śrāvaka* [vehicle].

"'Kāśyapa, if you can eat according to this [understanding] then you will not render void the charity of those who feed you.'

14. "At the time, World-honored One, the explanation I heard was unprecedented to me, and I immediately generated a profound sense of reverence for all bodhisattvas. I also thought, 'This householder's eloquence and wisdom being as they are, how could anyone who hears him not generate the intention to achieve *anuttarā samyaksambodhi*? From now on I will never exhort anyone to undertake the practices of *śrāvaka* or *pratyekabuddha*.' Therefore I cannot accept [your instruction] to go inquire about his illness."

15. The Buddha told Subhūti, "You go inquire about Vimala-kīrti's illness."

Subhūti addressed the Buddha, "World-honored One, I dare not accept your instruction to go inquire about his illness. Why? I remember once in the past, I entered into his home to beg. At the time Vimalakīrti filled my bowl full of food and said to me,

16. "'O Subhūti, if you are able to be universally same about eating, then the *dharma*s are also universally same; if the *dharma*s are universally same, you should also be universally same about eating. If you can practice begging like this, you may accept the food.

"'If, Subhūti, you refrain from eradicating licentiousness, anger, and stupidity, yet are not equipped with them; if you do not destroy the body, yet accord with the single characteristic; if you do not extinguish stupidity and affection, yet generate wisdom and eman-cipation; if you use the characteristics of the five transgressions to attain emancipation, without either emancipation or bondage; if you do not perceive the four noble truths, yet do not fail to per-ceive the truths; neither attaining the results [of becoming a stream-enterer (*srota-āpanna*), and so on,] nor not attaining the results; neither being an ordinary [unenlightened] person nor tran-scending the state (lit., "*dharma*") of ordinary person; neither being a sage nor not being a sage; accomplishing all the *dharma*s yet transcending the characteristics of the *dharma*s—then you can accept this food.

17. "'Subhūti, you should only accept this food if you can nei-ther see the Buddha nor hear the Dharma, nor the six teachers of heterodox paths—Pūraṇa Kāśyapa, Maskarin Gośālīputra, Saṃ-jayin Vairaṭīputra, Ajita Keśakambala, Kakuda Kātyāyana, and Nirgrantha Jñātiputra, who were your teachers, following whom you left home, [so that] at the defeat of those teachers you were also defeated—then you can accept this food.

18. "'If, Subhūti, you can enter into the heterodox views and not reach the other shore; abide in the eight difficulties and not attain the absence of difficulty; identify with the afflictions and

540c

transcend the pure *dharmas*; attain the *samādhi* of noncontention; if all sentient beings generate this concentration; if the donors do not name you their field of blessings; if those making offerings to you fall into the three evil destinations; if you join hands with the host of Māras and make them your co-workers; if you do not differentiate yourself from the host of Māras and the sensory troubles; if you bear resentment toward all sentient beings; if you revile the Buddhas, denigrate the Dharma, and do not enter the Sangha; and if you never attain extinction—if you are like this then you can accept the food.'

19. "When I heard these words, World-honored One, I was bewildered and did not understand what he had said. I did not know how to answer, so I put down the bowl and tried to leave his house. Vimalakīrti then said,

"'O Subhūti, do not be afraid to take your bowl. What is the meaning of this? If a [phantasmagorical] person whom the Tathāgata has created through the transformation [of conjury] is criticized for this, should he be afraid?' I said, 'No.' Vimalakīrti said, 'All the *dharmas* have the characteristic of being like phantasmagorical transformations. You should not have any fear now. Why? All verbal explanations do not transcend this characteristic. The wise are not attached to letters, and therefore they have no fear. Why? The nature of letters transcends [their characteristics]; there are no letters. This is emancipation, and the characteristic of emancipation is the *dharmas*.'

20. "When Vimalakīrti explained this Dharma, two hundred gods attained purification of their Dharma eyes. Therefore I cannot accept [your instruction] to go inquire about his illness."

21. The Buddha told Pūrṇamaitrāyaṇīputra, "You go inquire about Vimalakīrti's illness."

Pūrṇa addressed the Buddha, "World-honored One, I dare not accept your instruction to go inquire about his illness. Why? I remember once in the past, when I was beneath a tree in the forest explaining the Dharma to novice *bhikṣus*. At the time Vimalakīrti came and said to me,

22. "'O Pūrṇa, you should only explain the Dharma after first

entering into concentration and contemplating the minds of these people—do not put defiled food in a jeweled vessel. You should understand what these *bhikṣus* are thinking—do not put lapis lazuli together with crystal.

"'You are unable to understand the fundamental sources of sentient beings—do not inspire them with the Hinayana Dharma. Other and self are without flaw, so do not harm them. If someone wants to travel the great path (i.e., practice the Mahayana), do not show them a small pathway. The ocean cannot be contained within the hoofprint of an ox; the radiance of the sun cannot be equaled by that of a firefly.

541a

"'Pūrṇa, these *bhikṣus* have long since generated the aspiration for the Mahayana but in the midst [of many rebirths] they have forgotten this intention.

"'Why would you teach them with the Hinayana Dharma? When I consider the Hinayana, its wisdom is as minute as a blind man's, [and with it you are] unable to discriminate the sharp and dull faculties of all sentient beings.'

23. "Then Vimalakīrti entered into *samādhi* and made the *bhikṣus* aware of their previous lives. They had planted virtuous roots under five hundred Buddhas and had rededicated them to their [eventual achievement of] *anuttarā samyaksaṃbodhi*. [Learning this], they immediately experienced a suddenly expansive reacquisition of that original inspiration. At this the *bhikṣus* bowed their heads in reverence to Vimalakīrti's feet. Then Vimalakīrti explained the Dharma for them, and they never again retrogressed from [their progress to] *anuttarā samyaksaṃbodhi*.

24. "I thought, '*Śrāvaka*s do not consider the faculties of people and therefore should not explain the Dharma.'

"Therefore, I cannot accept [your instruction] to go inquire about his illness."

25. The Buddha told Mahākātyāyana, "You go inquire about Vimalakīrti's illness."

Kātyāyana addressed the Buddha, "World-honored One, I dare not accept your instruction to go inquire about his illness. Why? I remember once in the past, when the Buddha briefly explained the essentials of the Dharma to some *bhikṣu*s, and immediately afterward I expanded upon your meaning, discussing the meanings of impermanence, suffering, emptiness, no-self, and extinction. At the time Vimalakīrti came and said to me,

26. "'O Kātyāyana, do not explain the Dharma of the true characteristic using the mental processes of generation and extinction (i.e., samsara).

i) "'Kātyāyana, the *dharma*s are ultimately neither generated nor extinguished: this is the meaning of impermanence.

ii) "'The five *skandha*s are empty throughout, with no arising: this is the meaning of suffering.

iii) "'The *dharma*s ultimately do not exist: this is the meaning of emptiness.

iv) "'There is no self in the self, yet no duality: this is the meaning of no-self.

v) "'The *dharma*s were originally not burning and will not become extinguished now: this is the meaning of extinction.'

27. "When [Vimalakīrti] explained this Dharma, the *bhikṣu*s' minds attained emancipation. Therefore, I cannot accept [your instruction] to go inquire about his illness."

28. The Buddha told Aniruddha, "You go inquire about Vimalakīrti's illness."

Aniruddha addressed the Buddha, "World-honored One, I dare not accept your instruction to go inquire about his illness. Why?

29. "I remember once in the past I was walking quietly in a certain location. At the time a Brahmā king named Adorned Purity, in the company of ten thousand Brahmās generating pure radiance, proceeded to where I was. He bowed to my feet in reverence and asked me, 'How much, Aniruddha, can you see with your divine eye?'

"I answered, 'Sir, I see the trimegachiliocosm of Śākyamuni's Buddha land as if I were looking at a mango in the palm of my hand.'

541b   30. "Then Vimalakīrti came and said to me, 'O Aniruddha, is the seeing of the divine eye a constructed characteristic, or is it an unconstructed characteristic? If it is a constructed characteristic, then it is equivalent to the five supernormal powers of the heterodox paths. If it is an unconstructed characteristic then it is unconditioned and should be without seeing (i.e., "views").' World-honored One, at the time I remained silent.

31. "Hearing his words, the Brahmās attained something unprecedented, immediately reverenced [Vimalakīrti], and asked him, 'Who in this world has the true divine eye?' Vimalakīrti said, 'There is the Buddha, the World-honored One, who has attained the true divine eye. Always in *samādhi,* he sees all the Buddha lands without any characteristic of duality.'

32. "At this Adorned Purity Brahmā King and his attending five hundred Brahmā kings all generated the intention to achieve *anuttarā samyaksaṃbodhi.* They bowed to Vimalakīrti's feet, then instantly disappeared. Therefore, I cannot accept [your instruction] to go inquire about his illness."

33. The Buddha told Upāli, "You go inquire about Vimalakīrti's illness."

Upāli addressed the Buddha, "World-honored One, I dare not accept your instruction to go inquire about his illness. Why?

"I remember once in the past, there were two *bhikṣu*s who had violated the practice of the Vinaya but from their shame did not dare ask you about it. They came to ask me: 'O Upāli, we have violated the Vinaya and are sincerely ashamed, not daring to ask the Buddha about it. We want you to explain our doubts and the [need for] repentance, so that we may be relieved of the transgressions.' I immediately explained [the matter] to them according to the Dharma.

34. "At the time Vimalakīrti came and said to me,

"'O Upāli, do not increase these two *bhikṣu*s' transgressions. You should just remove [the transgressions] and not disturb their minds. Why?

"'The nature of those transgressions does not reside within, it does not reside without, and it does not reside in the middle.

"'As the Buddha has explained, when their minds are defiled, sentient beings are defiled. When their minds are purified, sentient beings are purified. The mind likewise does not reside within, does not reside without, and does not reside in the middle. Just so is the mind, and just so are transgression and defilement. The *dharmas* are also likewise, in not transcending suchness.

"'Just so, Upāli, when one attains emancipation using the characteristics of the mind, is it (i.e., the mind) defiled or not?' I said, 'It is not.'

"Vimalakīrti said, 'The characteristics of the minds of all sentient beings are likewise, in being without defilement.

35. "'O Upāli, to have false concepts is defilement; to be without false concepts is purity.

"'Confusion is defilement, and the absence of confusion is purity.

"'To grasp the self is defilement, and not to grasp the self is purity.

"'Upāli, all the *dharmas* are generated and extinguished, without abiding. Like phantasms or lightning bolts, the *dharmas* do not depend on each other. They do not abide even for a single instant. The *dharmas* are all false views, like a dream, like a mirage, like the moon [reflected] in water, like an image in a mirror—[all] generated from false conceptualization. Those who understand this are called "upholders of the Vinaya." Those who understand this are said to "understand well."'

541c   36. "At this the two *bhikṣus* said, 'Such superior wisdom! Upāli cannot match this! There could be no better explanation of upholding the Vinaya!'

"I then answered, 'Excluding the Tathāgata, there has never been a *śrāvaka* or bodhisattva able to command the eloquence for such a felicitous explanation—such is the brilliance of his wisdom!'

37. "At the time, the doubts and [need for] repentance of the two *bhikṣus* were eliminated. They generated the intention to achieve *anuttarā samyaksaṃbodhi,* speaking this vow: 'Let all sentient beings attain this [level of] eloquence!' Therefore, I cannot accept [your instruction] to go inquire about his illness."

38. The Buddha told Rāhula, "You go inquire about Vimalakīrti's illness."

Rāhula addressed the Buddha, "World-honored One, I dare not accept your instruction to go inquire about his illness. Why?

"I remember once in the past, the elders' sons of Vaiśālī came to where I was, bowed their heads to me in reverence, and asked, 'O Rāhula, you are the son of the Buddha, who forsook the position of universal ruler (*cakravartin*) and left home for the path (i.e., enlightenment). What benefits are there to leaving home?'

"I then explained to them, according to the Dharma, the benefits of the merits of leaving home. At that point Vimalakīrti came and said to me,

39. "'O Rāhula, you should not explain the benefits of the merits of leaving home. Why? To be without benefit and without merits—this is leaving home. One may explain that there are benefits and merits in the conditioned *dharma*s, but leaving home is an unconditioned *dharma* and there are no benefits and merits in unconditioned *dharma*s.

"'Rāhula, to leave home is to be without that and this, and without intermediate. It is to transcend the sixty-two views and be located in nirvana.

"'[Leaving home] is accepted by the wise and practiced by the sagely. It subjugates the host of Māras and [allows one to] transcend the five destinations, purify the five eyes, attain the five powers, and establish the five faculties. It is to be without vexation over "that," to transcend the host of heterogeneous evils, and to demolish the heterodox paths. It is to transcend provisional names and emerge from the muck [of samsara]. It is to be without attachments, without any sense of personal possession. It is to be without experience, without turmoil. It is to harbor joy within and defend the intentions of others. It is to accord with meditation and transcend the host of transgressions. If one can be like this, then this is true leaving home.'

40. "At this Vimalakīrti said to those elders' sons, 'You would do well to leave home together in the correct Dharma. Why? It is difficult to encounter a time when a Buddha is in the world.'

"The elders' sons said, 'O retired scholar, we have heard that the Buddha has said one may not leave home without first receiving permission from one's parents.'

"Vimalakīrti said, 'So it is. You should immediately generate the intention to achieve *anuttarā samyaksaṃbodhi,* and this is to "leave home." This is sufficient.'

41. "Then thirty-two elders' sons all generated the intention to achieve *anuttarā samyaksaṃbodhi.* Therefore, I cannot accept [your instruction] to go inquire about his illness."

542a

42. The Buddha told Ānanda, "You go inquire about Vimalakīrti's illness."

Ānanda addressed the Buddha, "World-honored One, I dare not accept your instruction to go inquire about his illness. Why? I remember once in the past, the World-honored One had a slight illness requiring cow's milk [as medicine]. I took my bowl and proceeded to the gateway of a great brahman home.

43. "While I was standing there Vimalakīrti came and said to me, 'O Ānanda, why are you standing here with your bowl so early in the morning?'

"I said, 'O retired scholar, the World-honored One has a slight illness requiring cow's milk, and so I have come here.'

"Vimalakīrti said, 'Stop, stop, Ānanda! Do not speak thus. The Tathāgata's body is the essence of *vajra.* [In it] the evils are already eradicated and the host of goods universally assembled. What illness could it have, what vexation could there be?

44. "'Go silently, Ānanda—do not revile the Tathāgata, and do not let anyone else hear such coarse talk. Do not allow the gods of awesome power and virtue and the bodhisattvas who have come from pure lands in other directions to hear these words.

"'Ānanda, even a small degree of blessings (i.e., merit) allows the wheel-turning sage king (*cakravartin*) to be without illness— how could the immeasurable blessings of the Tathāgata fail to exceed his in every regard?!

"'Go, Ānanda—do not make us experience this shame. If brahmans in the heterodox paths hear this, they will think, "Who is this teacher, who is unable to save himself from illness but would save others of their ills?" Sir, go in secret haste and do not let anyone hear this.

45. "'You should understand, Ānanda, the bodies of the Tathāgatas are bodies of the Dharma, not bodies of longing. The Buddha is the World-honored One, who has transcended the triple world. The Buddha's body is without flaws, the flaws having been extinguished. The Buddha's body is unconditioned and does not fit the [conventional] analytic categories. A body such as this—how could it be ill, how could it be vexed?'

46. "At the time, World-honored One, I was really ashamed that I might have mistakenly heard what the Buddha had said in spite of being so close.

"'I then heard a voice from space saying, 'Ānanda, it is as the retired scholar has said. It is just that the Buddha has appeared in this evil age of the five corruptions and manifests this Dharma to emancipate sentient beings. Go, Ānanda. Take the milk without shame.'

47. "World-honored One, the eloquence of Vimalakīrti's wisdom is like this. Therefore, I cannot accept [your instruction] to go inquire about his illness."

48. In similar fashion all of the Buddha's five hundred great disciples each explained their original encounters and related what Vimalakīrti had said, and each said he was unable to accept [the Buddha's instruction] to go inquire about [Vimalakīrti's] illness.

Chapter IV

Bodhisattvas

1. At this point the Buddha addressed Maitreya Bodhisattva, "You go inquire about Vimalakīrti's illness."

Maitreya addressed the Buddha, "World-honored One, I dare not accept your instruction to go inquire about his illness. Why? I remember once in the past when I was explaining the practice of ^{542b} the stage of irreversibility for the heavenly king of the Tuṣita Heaven and his subordinates. At the time Vimalakīrti came and said to me,

2. "'Maitreya, the World-honored One has bestowed on your noble person the prediction that you will achieve *anuttarā samyak-sambodhi* in a single lifetime. What lifetime will you use to experience this prediction, past, future, or present? If a past life, then the past life is already extinguished. If a future life, then the future life has not arrived. If the present life, then the present life is non-abiding. It is as the Buddha has explained, "O *bhikṣus*, you are in this immediate present born, aged, and extinguished."

"'If you experience this prediction with birthlessness, then the birthless is the primary status [of Hinayanist enlightenment]. Yet within that primary status there is no receiving the prediction, and also no attainment of *anuttarā samyaksambodhi*.

3. "'How, Maitreya, did you receive the prediction of [Buddhahood in] a single lifetime? Did you receive the prediction from the generation of suchness, or did you receive the prediction from the extinction of suchness?

"'If you received the prediction by the generation of suchness, then [understand that] suchness is without generation. If you received the prediction by the extinction of suchness, then [understand that] suchness is without extinction.

"'All sentient beings are entirely suchlike, and all *dharma*s are also entirely suchlike. The assembly of sages and wise ones are also suchlike. Even you, Maitreya, are suchlike. If you received the prediction [of future Buddhahood], all sentient beings should also receive it. Why? Suchness is nondual and nondifferentiated. If Maitreya attains *anuttarā samyaksaṃbodhi,* then all sentient beings should also all attain it. Why? All sentient beings are the characteristic of *bodhi.* If Maitreya attains extinction, then all sentient beings should also all [attain] extinction. Why? The Buddhas understand that all sentient beings are ultimately extinguished, which is the characteristic of nirvana, and cannot again be extinguished.

"'Therefore, Maitreya, do not inspire the gods with this teaching.

4. "'Truly, there is no one who generates the intention to achieve *anuttarā samyaksaṃbodhi,* and there is no one who retrogresses. Maitreya, you should have these gods forsake this discriminative view of *bodhi.* Why?

"'*Bodhi* cannot be attained with the body, and it cannot be attained with the mind.

"'Extinction is *bodhi,* because of the extinction of the characteristics.

"'Non-contemplation is *bodhi,* because it transcends the conditions.

"'Non-practice is *bodhi,* because it is without recollection.

"'Eradication is *bodhi,* because of renouncing the views. Transcendence is *bodhi,* because of the transcendence of false concepts.

"'Hindrances are *bodhi,* because of the hindrance of the vows.

"'Non-entry is *bodhi,* because of the absence of lustful attachment. Accordance is *bodhi,* because of accordance with suchness.

"'Abiding is *bodhi,* because of abiding [in the] Dharma-nature.

"'Approach is *bodhi,* because of the approach to the reality-limit.

"'Nonduality is *bodhi,* because of the transcendence of mind and *dharma*s.

"'Universal sameness is *bodhi,* because of universal sameness with space.

"'The unconditioned is *bodhi,* because of the absence of generation, abiding, and extinction.

"'Understanding is *bodhi,* because of the comprehension of the mental processes of sentient beings.

"'Non-assemblage is *bodhi,* because of the non-assemblage of the entrances (*āyatana*s, i.e., sensory capacities).

"'Non-aggregation is *bodhi,* because of the transcendence of the latent influences of the afflictions.

"'The non-locative is *bodhi,* because of formlessness.

"'Provisional names are *bodhi,* because names are empty.

"'The [activities of the] conversion of suchness are *bodhi,* because of the nonexistence of grasping and forsaking.

"'The non-turbulent is *bodhi,* because of permanent composure.

"'Good serenity is *bodhi,* because of the purity of the natures.

"'Non-grasping is *bodhi,* because of the transcendence of objectified mentation.

"'Nondifferentiation is *bodhi,* because of the universal sameness of the *dharma*s.

"'Non-comparison is *bodhi,* because of the impossibility of analogy.

"'The subtle is *bodhi,* because of the difficulty of understanding the *dharma*s.'

5. "World-honored One, when Vimalakīrti explained this Dharma, two hundred gods achieved the forbearance of the non-arising of *dharma*s. Therefore, I cannot accept [your instruction] to go inquire about his illness."

6. The Buddha told Radiance Ornament Youth, "You go inquire about Vimalakīrti's illness."

Radiance Ornament Youth addressed the Buddha, "World-honored One, I dare not accept your instruction to go inquire about his illness. Why? I remember once in the past, when I was coming out of the great city of Vaiśālī just as Vimalakīrti was entering the city. I immediately bowed and asked, 'Retired scholar, from where are you coming?'

"He answered me, 'I have come from the place of enlightenment.'

"I asked, 'Where is the place of enlightenment?'

"He answered,

7. "'Sincerity is the place of enlightenment, because of the absence of falsity. The generation of practice is the place of enlightenment, because it is able to discriminate things. Profound mind is the place of enlightenment, because of the increase in merit. The mind of *bodhi* (*bodhicitta*) is the place of enlightenment, because of the absence of error.

8. "'Charity is the place of enlightenment, because of not seeking after retribution (i.e., reward). Morality is the place of enlightenment, because of the fulfillment of vows. Forbearance is the place of enlightenment, because of the absence of any mental hindrance regarding sentient beings. Exertion is the place of enlightenment, because of not retrogressing. Meditation is the place of enlightenment, because of the pliable disciplining of the mind. Wisdom is the place of enlightenment, because of the manifest perception of the *dharma*s.

9. "'Sympathy is the place of enlightenment, because of the universal sameness of sentient beings. Compassion is the place of enlightenment, because of the forbearance of suffering. Joy is the place of enlightenment, because of taking pleasure in the Dharma. Equanimity is the place of enlightenment, because of the eradication of repugnance and affection.

10. "'The numinous penetrations are the place of enlightenment, because of the achievement of the six penetrations (i.e., supernatural abilities). Emancipation is the place of enlightenment, because of the ability to forsake. Skillful means are the place of enlightenment, because of the salvation of sentient beings. The four means of attraction are the place of enlightenment, because of the attraction (i.e., conversion) of sentient beings. Erudition is the place of enlightenment, because of practice according to one's

knowledge. Mental control is the place of enlightenment, because of the correct contemplation of the *dharma*s. The thirty-seven factors of enlightenment are the place of enlightenment, because of forsaking the conditioned *dharma*s. The truth is the place of enlightenment, because of not misleading the world.

"'Conditioned generation is the place of enlightenment, because ignorance and so forth through old age and death, are all unexhausted. The afflictions are *bodhi,* because of understanding according to actuality.

11. "'Sentient beings are the place of enlightenment, because of understanding no-self.

"'All *dharma*s are the place of enlightenment, because of understanding the emptiness of the *dharma*s. Subjugation of the Māras is the place of enlightenment, because of not being swayed. The triple world is the place of enlightenment, because of the absence of destinations. The lion's roar is the place of enlightenment, because of the absence of fear. The [ten] powers, [four] fearlessnesses, and [eighteen] exclusive attributes are the place of enlightenment, because of the absence of transgressions. The three illuminations are the place of enlightenment, because of the absence of remaining hindrances. To understand all the *dharma*s in a single moment of thought is the place of enlightenment, because of the accomplishment of omniscience.

12. "'Thus, my good man, should the bodhisattva teach sentient beings according to the perfections. In all that is done, [down to every] lifting or placing of one's foot, you should understand that all these come from the place of enlightenment and abide in the Buddha-Dharma.'

13. "When [Vimalakīrti] explained the Dharma five hundred gods and humans all generated the intention to achieve *anuttarā samyaksaṃbodhi*. Therefore, I cannot accept [your instruction] to go inquire about his illness."

14. The Buddha told Maintains the World Bodhisattva, "You go inquire about Vimalakīrti's illness."

Maintains the World addressed the Buddha, "World-honored One, I dare not accept your instruction to go inquire about his illness. Why?

"I remember once in the past when I was residing in a meditation chamber, Māra the Evil One, attended by twelve thousand goddesses and in a manner like Indra with his drum, music, and song, proceeded to where I was. He and his subordinates bowed their heads to my feet, held their palms together reverentially, and stood to one side.

"Thinking it was Indra, I said to him, 'Welcome, Kauśika! Although [you enjoy] blessings you should not be self-indulgent. You should contemplate the impermanence of the five desires and seek for the foundation of goodness, cultivating the perduring *dharma*s with regard to your body, life, and wealth.'

"He then said to me, 'O good sir, [please] receive these twelve thousand goddesses to clean and wash [for you].'

"I said, 'Kauśika, as a *śramaṇa* and son of Śākya I have no need for improper things such as this. This would not be appropriate for me.'

15. "Before I had even finished saying this Vimalakīrti came and said to me, 'This is not Indra. This is Māra, who has come only to ridicule you.'

"He then said to Māra, 'You can give these women to me. If it were I, I would accept them.'

"Māra then thought in shock, 'Vimalakīrti should not be troubling me!' He wanted to become invisible and leave but he could not disappear. Even using all his numinous power he was not able to leave.

"He then heard a voice from space, saying, 'Evil One, if you give him the women you will be able to go.'

"Because of his fear, and with eyes casting nervously about, [Māra] gave Vimalakīrti the women.

16. "Then Vimalakīrti said to the women, 'Māra has given you to me. You should now all generate the intention to achieve *anuttarā samyaksaṃbodhi*.'

"He then explained the Dharma to them in various ways and caused them to generate the intention for enlightenment.

"He then said, 'Now that you have generated the intention for enlightenment, you may amuse yourselves in the joy of the Dharma, never again taking pleasure in the five desires.'

"The goddesses asked, 'What is the joy of the Dharma?'

"He answered, 'Joy is to always trust the Buddha. Joy is to 543b desire to hear the Dharma. Joy is to make offerings to the assembly. Joy is to transcend the five desires. Joy is to contemplate the five *skandha*s as vengeful bandits. Joy is to contemplate the four elements as poisonous snakes. Joy is to contemplate the interior sensory capacities as being like empty aggregations. Joy is to maintain one's intention for enlightenment in all situations. Joy is to benefit sentient beings. Joy is to revere teachers. Joy is the extensive practice of charity. Joy is the firm maintenance of the precepts. Joy is forbearance and pliability. Joy is the vigorous accumulation of good roots. Joy is the lack of disturbance in meditation. Joy is to transcend the defilements in wisdom. Joy is to disseminate *bodhicitta*. Joy is the subjugation of the host of Māras. Joy is the eradication of the afflictions. Joy is purification of the countries of the Buddhas. Joy is the accomplishment of the [thirty-two primary] characteristics and [eighty subsidiary] marks, based on the cultivation of the merits. Joy is ornamentation of the place of enlightenment. Joy is to hear the profound Dharma without fear. Joy is the three emancipations and not to take the pleasure [of ultimate enlightenment] at an inappropriate time. Joy is to associate with fellow trainees. Joy is for one's mind to be without hindrance in the midst of those [who are] not one's fellow trainees. Joy is to defend against evil friends. Joy is to associate closely with good friends. Joy is to be happy and pure in mind. Joy is to cultivate the immeasurable factors of enlightenment.

"'These are the bodhisattva's joy in the Dharma.'

17. "At this Māra the Evil One announced to the women, 'I want to return with you to the heavenly palace.'

"The women said, 'You already gave us to this retired scholar. We are extremely joyful in the joy of the Dharma, and will never again take pleasure in the five desires.'

"Māra said, 'If the retired scholar is able to forsake these women, and everything that exists is given to him, then he is a bodhisattva.'

"Vimalakīrti said, 'I have already forsaken them. You may take them away, but you must make all sentient beings attain fulfillment of their vows in the Dharma.'

"At this the women asked Vimalakīrti, 'How should we reside in Māra's palace?'

18. "Vimalakīrti said, 'Sisters, there is a Dharma called "inexhaustible lamp." You should study it. The inexhaustible lamp is like a lamp that ignites a hundred thousand lamps, illuminating all darkness with an illumination that is never exhausted. Thus, sisters, if a single bodhisattva guides a hundred thousand sentient beings, causing them to generate the intention to achieve *anuttarā samyaksaṃbodhi,* that bodhisattva's intention to achieve enlightenment will also never be extinguished.

"'With each teaching of the Dharma all the good *dharma*s are naturally increased. This is what is called the "inexhaustible lamp." Although you reside in Māra's palace, with this inexhaustible lamp you can cause innumerable gods and goddesses to generate the intention to achieve *anuttarā samyaksaṃbodhi.* Thereby you will repay the Buddha's kindness and also greatly benefit all sentient beings.'

19. "At that time the goddesses bowed their heads to Vimalakīrti's feet in worship and suddenly disappeared to return to Māra's palace.

"World-honored One, Vimalakīrti's autonomy, numinous power, wisdom, and eloquence are like this. Therefore, I cannot accept [your instruction] to go inquire about his illness."

543c

20. The Buddha told the elder's son Good Virtue, "You go inquire about Vimalakīrti's illness."

Good Virtue addressed the Buddha, "World-honored One, I dare not accept your instruction to go inquire about his illness. Why?

116

"I remember once in the past when I was holding a great charity assembly in my father's house. We made offerings to all the *śramaṇa*s, brahmans, those of the heterodox paths, the poor, low-class, orphans, and beggars. It lasted fully seven days. At the time Vimalakīrti came into the assembly and said to me, 'Elder's son, you should not hold a great charity assembly like this. You should have an assembly of the charity of the Dharma. What use is a charity assembly of material wealth?'

"I said, 'Retired scholar, what is an assembly of the charity of Dharma?'

"He answered,

21. "'An assembly of the charity of the Dharma is to make offerings to all sentient beings simultaneously, without before and after. This is called an assembly of the charity of the Dharma.

"'If you ask how I say this, I say that one uses *bodhi* to generate sympathy. One generates great compassion in order to save sentient beings. One generates joy by maintaining the correct Dharma. One practices equanimity by mastering wisdom.

22. "'One generates *dāna-pāramitā* (the perfection of charity) by mastering desire. One generates *śīla-pāramitā* (the perfection of morality) by attracting those who transgress the precepts. One generates *kṣanti-pāramitā* (the perfection of forbearance) by the Dharma of no-self. One generates *vīrya-pāramitā* (the perfection of exertion) by transcending the characteristics of body and mind. One generates *dhyāna-pāramitā* (the perfection of meditation) with the characteristic of *bodhi*. One generates *prajñā-pāramitā* (the perfection of wisdom) with omniscience.

23. "'One teaches sentient beings and generates emptiness. Without forsaking the conditioned *dharma*s, one generates that which is without characteristics. One manifests the experience of [re]birth and generates the uncreated.

24. "'One defends the correct Dharma and generates the power of skillful means. One generates the four means of attraction by saving sentient beings. One generates the elimination of conceit by reverencing all. One generates the three perduring *dharma*s with

regard to body, life, and wealth. One generates contemplation of the *dharma*s within the six mindfulnesses. One generates sincerity with regard to the six types of considerate esteem. One generates pure livelihood with correct practice of the good *dharma*s. One becomes close to the wise and sagely with purification of the mind in joy. One generates a disciplined mind by not having aversion for bad people. One generates the profound mind with the *dharma* of leaving home. One generates erudition by practicing according to the explanation. One generates the locus of empty repose with the *dharma* of noncontention. In approaching Buddha wisdom one generates sitting in repose. In releasing the bonds of sentient beings one generates the stages of cultivation.

25. "'By becoming replete in the [thirty-two primary] characteristics and [eighty subsidiary] marks and by purifying a Buddha land one generates meritorious karma. Understanding the thoughts of all sentient beings and how one should explain the Dharma to them, one generates the karma of wisdom. Understanding all the *dharma*s, one neither grasps nor forsakes. Entering the gate of the single characteristic, one generates the karma of sagacity. Eradicating all the afflictions, all the hindrances, and all the nongood *dharma*s, one generates all good karma.

26. "'By attaining omniscience and all the good *dharma*s, one universally generates the *dharma*s that assist one's Buddhahood. Thus, good man, is the assembly of the charity of the Dharma. If a bodhisattva resides in this assembly of the charity of the Dharma he will be a great donor. He will also be a field of blessings for the entire world.'

544a

"World-honored One, when Vimalakīrti explained this Dharma, two hundred people in the congregation of brahmans all generated the intention to achieve *anuttarā samyaksaṃbodhi*.

27. "At the time my own mind attained a purity which I exclaimed to be unprecedented, and I bowed my head to Vimalakīrti's feet in worship. Unfastening my necklace, a hundred thousand [coins] in value, I gave it to him but he did not accept it. I said, 'Please, retired scholar, you must accept this and give it to

whomever you please.' Vimalakīrti then accepted the necklace and divided it into two parts. Taking one part, he gave it to the lowliest beggars in the assembly. Taking the other part, he offered it to the Tathāgata Difficult to Overcome. The entire assembly saw the Radiant Illumination country and Difficult to Overcome Tathāgata. They also saw the necklace on that Buddha change into a four-pillared jewel-laden platform, with mutually noninterfering ornamentation on the four sides.

28. "Having manifested these numinous transformations, Vimalakīrti then said, 'If a donor with an attitude of universal sameness gives to the lowliest beggars, this is to be like the characteristic of the Tathāgata's field of blessings, with no distinction, and to be equivalent to great compassion without seeking any reward. This is called "to be replete in the charity of the Dharma."'

29. "The lowliest beggars in the city witnessed this numinous power and heard his explanation, and they all generated the intention to achieve *anuttarā samyaksambodhi*.

"Therefore, I cannot accept [your instruction] to go inquire about his illness."

30. In similar fashion all of the bodhisattvas explained their original encounters and related what Vimalakīrti had said, and each said he was unable to accept [the Buddha's instruction] to go inquire about his illness.

End of Fascicle One

Fascicle Two

Chapter V

Mañjuśrī's Condolence Visit

1. At this point the Buddha addressed Mañjuśrī, "You go inquire about Vimalakīrti's illness."

Mañjuśrī addressed the Buddha, "World-honored One, that superior one is difficult to respond to.

"He has profoundly attained the true characteristic, and he is good at explaining the essentials of the Dharma.

"His eloquence is unhampered, and his wisdom is unhindered.

"He completely understands all the deportments of the bodhisattvas, and he has entered into all the secret storehouses of the Buddhas.

"He has subjugated the host of Māras, and disports himself in the numinous penetrations. He has already attained perfection in his wisdom and skillful means.

"Nevertheless, I will accept your sagely purport and proceed to inquire about his illness."

2. Thereupon the bodhisattvas, great disciples, Indras, Brahmās, and the four heavenly kings in the assembly all thought, "Now these two great bodhisattvas Mañjuśrī and Vimalakīrti will have a discussion. They will certainly explain a wondrous Dharma."

At the time eight thousand bodhisattvas, five hundred śrāvakas, and a hundred thousand gods all wanted to follow along.

Mañjuśrī and the congregation of bodhisattvas and great

disciples, with the gods reverentially surrounding them, then entered the great city of Vaiśālī.

3. At that time the Elder Vimalakīrti thought, "Now Mañjuśrī and a great congregation is coming."

Then with his numinous power he emptied out his room, removing what was there as well as his servants. He left only a single couch, upon which he reclined in his illness.

4. Mañjuśrī entered the house, and he saw the room was empty, with [Vimalakīrti] lying alone on a single couch.

Then Vimalakīrti said, "Welcome, Mañjuśrī. You have come with the characteristic of not coming; you see with the characteristic of not seeing."

Mañjuśrī said, "So it is, retired scholar. If one has come, there is no more coming. If one has gone, there is no more going. Why? To come is to come from nowhere; to go is to proceed nowhere. That which can be seen is then invisible.

5. "But enough of this matter. Retired scholar, can this illness be forborn? In its treatment is it diminished, so as not to increase? The World-honored One has made immeasurable courteous inquiries about you.

6. "Retired scholar, what is the cause from which this illness arises? Has it been affecting you long? How will it be extinguished?"

Vimalakīrti said, "From stupidity there is affection, and hence the generation of my illness (or: the illness of self). Since all sentient beings are ill, therefore I am ill. If the illness of all sentient beings were extinguished, then my illness would be extinguished. Why? Bodhisattvas enter samsara on behalf of sentient beings. Because there is samsara, there is illness. If sentient beings were able to transcend illness, then bodhisattvas would not also be ill.

7. "It is like an elder whose only son becomes ill, and the parents become ill as well. If the son recovers from the illness, the parents also recover. Bodhisattvas are like this. They have affection for sentient beings as if for their own children. When sentient beings are ill the bodhisattvas are ill also, and when sentient beings recover from their illness the bodhisattvas recover also."

He also said, "From what cause does this illness arise? The illness of bodhisattvas arises from great compassion."

8. Mañjuśrī said, "Retired scholar, why is this room empty, with no servants?"

Vimalakīrti said, "The countries of the Buddhas are also all empty." 544c

[Mañjuśrī] asked, "With what was it emptied?"

[Vimalakīrti] answered, "It was emptied with emptiness."

[Mañjuśrī] asked further, "How can emptiness use emptiness?"

[Vimalakīrti] answered, "It is empty through nondiscriminating emptiness."

[Mañjuśrī] asked further, "Can emptiness be discriminated?"

[Vimalakīrti] answered, "Discrimination is also empty."

[Mañjuśrī] asked further, "Where should emptiness be sought?"

[Vimalakīrti] answered, "It should be sought within the sixty-two [heterodox] views."

[Mañjuśrī] asked further, "Where should the sixty-two views be sought?"

[Vimalakīrti] answered, "They should be sought within the emancipation of the Buddhas."

[Mañjuśrī] asked further, "Where should the emancipation of the Buddhas be sought?"

[Vimalakīrti] answered, "It should be sought within the mental processes of all sentient beings.

"Also, regarding your question about why there are no servants—all the host of Māras and [followers of] the heterodox paths are all my servants. Why? The host of Māras take pleasure in samsara, and the bodhisattvas do not forsake samsara. Those of the heterodox paths take pleasure in the views, and bodhisattvas are unmoved by the views."

9. Mañjuśrī said, "Retired scholar, what characteristics does your illness have?"

Vimalakīrti said, "My illness is without form, invisible."

[Mañjuśrī] asked further, "Is this an illness of body or of mind?"

[Vimalakīrti] said, "It is not of the body, since the body transcends characteristics. Nor is it of the mind, since the mind is like a phantasm."

[Mañjuśrī] asked further, "Of the four elements of earth, water, fire, and air, to which element does this illness belong?"

[Vimalakīrti] answered, "This illness is not of the earth element, but neither does it transcend the earth element. The water, fire, and wind elements are likewise. However, the illnesses of sentient beings arise from the four elements, and because they are ill I am ill."

10. At that time Mañjuśrī asked Vimalakīrti, "How should bodhisattvas comfort bodhisattvas who are ill?"

Vimalakīrti said, "Explain that the body is impermanent but do not teach that one should have aversion for one's body. Explain that the body suffers but do not teach that one should take pleasure in nirvana. Explain that the body is without self but teach that one should guide sentient beings [anyway]. Explain that the body is emptily serene but do not teach that it is ultimately extinguished.

"Explain that one should regret one's former transgressions but do not teach that they enter into the past. Comfort the illness of others with one's own illness. One should recognize the innumerable *kalpa*s of suffering of one's past lives. One should be mindful of benefiting all sentient beings and remember one's cultivation of blessings, be mindful of one's pure livelihood without generating vexation but always generating exertion. Be the physician king, healing the host of illnesses. Thus should bodhisattvas comfort bodhisattvas who are ill, making them happy."

11. Mañjuśrī said, "Retired scholar, how should the bodhisattva who is ill control his mind?"

Vimalakīrti said, "The bodhisattva who is ill should think as follows:

"'This present illness of mine comes entirely from the false concepts, confusions, and afflictions of previous lives. There is no actual *dharma* that experiences illness.'

"Why? 'Body' is a provisional name for a conglomeration of the four elements, and the four elements have no master.

"The body also has no self. Furthermore, the arising of this illness is entirely due to attachment to self. Therefore, one should not generate attachment regarding the self. You should understand that this is the foundation of illness and so eliminate the conception of 'self' and the conception of 'sentient being.'

"You should give rise to the conception of *dharmas*, thinking as follows: 'It is only through the combination of a host of *dharmas* that this body is created. Its arising is only the arising of *dharmas*, and its extinction is only the extinction of *dharmas*.' Also, 'these *dharmas* do not know themselves. When they arise, they do not say "I have arisen." When they are extinguished, they do not say "I have become extinguished."'

12. "The bodhisattva who is ill should undertake the conception (or: visualization) of the extinguished *dharmas*. He should think as follows, 'This conception of the *dharmas* is also a confused [view]. Such a confused [view] is a great calamity, and I should transcend it.' What should be transcended? One should transcend the self and [the sense of] personal possession. What is it to transcend the self and [the sense of] personal possession? It is to transcend the two *dharmas*. What is it to transcend the two *dharmas*? It is to be mindful neither of interior nor exterior *dharmas* and to practice universal sameness. What is universal sameness? It is for self to be same and for nirvana to be same. Why? Both self and nirvana are empty. Why are they empty? They are merely names, and therefore empty. Thus these two *dharmas* are without definitive nature. When one attains universal sameness there is no remaining illness. There is only the illness of emptiness, and the illness of emptiness is also empty.

13. "Bodhisattvas who are ill should use nonexperience to experience the experiences. They acquire realization without becoming complete in the *dharmas* of Buddhahood and without extinguishing experience. Given the suffering of their bodies, they think of sentient beings in the evil destinations and generate great compassion, [thinking] 'I have already controlled [my suffering] and I should also control [the suffering] of all sentient beings.'

14. "Just eliminate the illness; do not eliminate *dharma*s. [Bodhisattvas] teach [sentient beings] so that they eliminate the basis of their illness.

"What is the basis of their illness? It is the presence of objectified mentation. It is through objectified mentation that the basis of illness is constituted.

"What is objectified mentation? It is the triple world. What is it to eliminate objectified mentation? It is done with nonattainment.

"If there is no attainment, there is no objectified mentation. What is nonattainment? It is the transcendence of dualistic views.

"What are dualistic views? They are the internalistic view and externalistic view. These are without attainment (i.e., not apprehensible).

"Mañjuśrī, this is how bodhisattvas who are ill control their minds. This is how they eliminate old age, illness, death, and suffering. This is the bodhisattva's *bodhi*. If it were not like this, then my cultivation would be a foolish waste. It is like one who is victorious over his enemies being called a hero: this is the term for the bodhisattva who has simultaneously eliminated old age, illness, and death.

15. "Bodhisattvas who are ill should think as follows: 'If this illness of mine is neither real nor existent, then the illnesses of sentient beings are also neither real nor existent.'

"When performing this contemplation, [such bodhisattvas] may generate an affectionate view of great compassion with regard to (i.e., sentimental compassion toward) sentient beings, but this should be forsaken. Why?

"Bodhisattvas eliminate the vexations of sensory data and generate great compassion. If they have an affectionate view of compassion, they would thereby generate aversion toward samsara. If they are able to transcend this they will not have any [such] aversion, and no matter where they are subsequently reborn they will not be limited by any affectionate view. They will be born without bonds and be able to explain the Dharma to sentient beings and emancipate them from their bonds.

545b

"It is as the Buddha has explained: 'It is impossible for someone with bonds to emancipate others from their bonds. It is only possible for someone without bonds to emancipate others from their bonds.' Therefore, bodhisattvas should not generate bonds.

16. "What are bonds, and what is emancipation?

"A desirous attachment to the flavor of meditation is the bond of bodhisattvas; and birth through skillful means is the emancipation of bodhisattvas.

"Further, to be without skillful means is to have one's wisdom in bondage, while to have skillful means is to have one's wisdom emancipated.

"To be without wisdom is to have one's skillful means in bondage, while to have wisdom is to have one's skillful means emancipated.

17. "What is it to be without skillful means and one's wisdom in bondage? It is for bodhisattvas to use affection to ornament the Buddha lands and accomplish [the salvation of] sentient beings, to control oneself within [the three emancipations of] emptiness, signlessness, and wishlessness. This is called being without skillful means and one's wisdom in bondage.

"What is it to have skillful means with one's wisdom emancipated? It is not to use affection to ornament the Buddha lands and accomplish [the liberation of] sentient beings, and to control oneself so as to be without aversion within [the three emancipations of] emptiness, signlessness, and wishlessness. This is called having skillful means with one's wisdom emancipated.

"What is it to be without wisdom and have one's skillful means in bondage? It is for bodhisattvas to plant a host of virtuous roots while abiding in the afflictions of desire, anger, and false views. This is called being without wisdom with one's skillful means in bondage.

"What is it to have wisdom with one's skillful means emancipated? It is to transcend the afflictions of desire, anger, and false views and plant a host of virtuous roots, rededicating [the merit to one's achievement of] *anuttarā samyaksaṃbodhi*. This is called having wisdom with one's skillful means emancipated.

18. "Mañjuśrī, bodhisattvas who are ill should contemplate the *dharmas* like this:

"Also, to contemplate the body as impermanent, suffering, empty, and no-self is called wisdom.

"Although the body is ill, it always exists in samsara. To benefit all without tiring—this is called skillful means.

"Also, in contemplating the body, [one should realize] that the body does not transcend illness and illness does not transcend the body, and that this illness and this body are neither new nor old—this is called wisdom. For one's body to be ill but never die is called skillful means.

19. "Mañjuśrī, thus should bodhisattvas who are ill control the mind. They should not abide within [the controlled mind], and they should also not abide in the uncontrolled mind. Why? To abide in the uncontrolled mind is the Dharma of fools. To abide in the controlled mind is the Dharma of *śrāvakas*. Therefore, bodhisattvas should not abide in either the controlled or uncontrolled mind. To transcend these two Dharmas is the practice of bodhisattvas. To be within samsara and not undertake polluted practices, to abide in nirvana and never become extinguished: this is the practice of bodhisattvas.

20. i) "It is neither the practice of ordinary [unenlightened persons] nor the practice of the wise and sagely: this is the practice of bodhisattvas.

545c   ii) "It is neither a defiled practice nor a pure practice: this is the practice of bodhisattvas.

iii) "Although in the past one [performed] the practices of Māra, in the present one subjugates the host of Māras: this is the practice of bodhisattvas.

iv) "To seek omniscience but not to seek it at the improper time: this is the practice of bodhisattvas.

v) "Although one contemplates the *dharmas* as nongenerated, not to enter the primary status [of Buddhahood]: this is the practice of bodhisattvas.

vi) "Although one contemplates the twelve [factors of] conditioned generation, to enter the heterodox views: this is the practice of bodhisattvas.

vii) "Although one attracts all sentient beings, to be without the attachment of affection: this is the practice of bodhisattvas.

viii) "Although one takes pleasure in transcendence, not to rely on the elimination of body and mind: this is the practice of bodhisattvas.

ix) "Although one practices [throughout] the triple world, not to destroy the Dharma-nature: this is the practice of bodhisattvas.

x) "Although practicing [the emancipation of] emptiness, to plant the host of virtuous roots: this is the practice of bodhisattvas.

xi) "Although practicing [the emancipation of] signlessness, to save sentient beings: this is the practice of bodhisattvas.

xii) "Although practicing [the emancipation of] wishlessness, to manifest the experience of a body: this is the practice of bodhisattvas.

xiii) "Although practicing nonactivation, to activate all good practices: this is the practice of bodhisattvas.

xiv) "Although practicing the six *pāramitā*s (perfections), to universally understand the minds and mental attributes of sentient beings: this is the practice of bodhisattvas.

xv) "Although practicing the six penetrations, not to exhaust the flaws: this is the practice of bodhisattvas.

xvi) "Although practicing the four unlimited states of mind, not to desire birth in the Brahmā world: this is the practice of bodhisattvas.

xvii) "Although practicing concentration, meditation, emancipation, and *samādhi,* not to be born [in a corresponding heaven] according to one's concentration: this is the practice of bodhisattvas.

xviii) "Although practicing the four foundations of mindfulness, never to transcend the body, sensation, mind, and *dharmas*: this is the practice of bodhisattvas.

xix) "Although practicing the four right efforts, not to forsake exertion of body and mind: this is the practice of bodhisattvas.

xx) "Although practicing the four supernormal abilities, to attain autonomy in numinous penetration: this is the practice of bodhisattvas.

xxi) "Although practicing [in the context of] the five faculties, to discriminate the sharp and dull faculties of all sentient beings: this is the practice of bodhisattvas.

xxii) "Although practicing the five powers, to delight in seeking the ten powers of a Buddha: this is the practice of bodhisattvas.

xxiii) "Although practicing the seven factors of enlightenment, to discriminate Buddha wisdom: this is the practice of bodhisattvas.

xxiv) "Although practicing the eightfold noble path, to take pleasure in practicing the unlimited path[s] to Buddhahood: this is the practice of bodhisattvas.

xxv) "Although practicing concentration and contemplation, the auxiliary factors of the path, yet ultimately never to fall into extinction: this is the practice of bodhisattvas.

xxvi) "Although practicing [with an awareness of] the non-generation and nonextinction of the *dharmas*, to ornament one's body with the [thirty-two primary] characteristics and [eighty subsidiary] marks: this is the practice of bodhisattvas.

xxvii) "Although manifesting the deportment of a *śrāvaka* or *pratyekabuddha,* not to forsake the Buddha-Dharma: this is the practice of bodhisattvas.

xxviii) "Although being in accord with the ultimate characteristic of the purity of the *dharmas*, to manifest one's body where needed: this is the practice of bodhisattvas.

xxix) "Although contemplating the Buddhas' countries as permanently serene like space, yet to manifest the various pure Buddha lands: this is the practice of bodhisattvas.

xxx) "Although attaining the enlightenment of Buddhahood, turning the wheel of the Dharma, and entering nirvana, yet not to forsake the bodhisattva path: this is the practice of bodhisattvas."

When [Vimalakīrti] explained [the Dharma] in these words, eight thousand gods within the great assembly led by Mañjuśrī all generated the intention to achieve *anuttarā samyaksaṃbodhi.*

546a

Chapter VI

Inconceivable

1. At this point Śāriputra saw that there were no seats in the room. He thought, "Where will this congregation of bodhisattvas and great disciples sit?"

The Elder Vimalakīrti knew what he was thinking and said to Śāriputra, "Which is it, sir—did you come for the Dharma or come seeking a seat?"

Śāriputra said, "I came for the Dharma, not for a seat."

2. Vimalakīrti said, "O Śāriputra, those who seek the Dharma should begrudge neither body nor life. How much more so a seat!

"To seek the Dharma is not a seeking in the context of form, sensation, concept, processes, and consciousness, nor a seeking in the context of the realms (dhātus) and entrances (āyatanas).

"[To seek the Dharma] is not a seeking in the context of [the three realms of] desire, form, and formlessness.

3. "O Śāriputra, in seeking the Dharma one should not be attached to the Buddha in seeking, nor be attached to the Dharma in seeking, nor be attached to the congregation [of the Sangha] in seeking. In seeking the Dharma, one should seek without recognizing suffering, one should seek without cutting off the accumulation [of suffering], one should seek without contriving the complete realization and cultivation of the path. Why? The Dharma is without contrived theories. If one says 'I will recognize suffering, cut off the accumulation [of suffering], and realize the extinction [of suffering] and cultivate the path,' this would be a contrived theory and not to seek the Dharma.

"O Śāriputra, the Dharma is named extinction: if one practices generation and extinction this is to seek generation and extinction, not to seek the Dharma.

"The Dharma is named the undefiled: if the *dharmas*, up to and including nirvana, are defiled, then this is defiled attachment and not to seek the Dharma.

"The Dharma is without any locus of its practice: if one practices in the Dharma, this is a locus of practice and not to seek the Dharma.

"The Dharma is without grasping and forsaking: if one grasps and forsakes the Dharma, then this is grasping and forsaking and not to seek the Dharma.

4. "The Dharma is without locus: if one is attached to locus, this is to be attached to locus and not to seek the Dharma.

"The Dharma is named 'without characteristics': if one's understanding accords with characteristics, this is to seek characteristics and not to seek the Dharma.

"One cannot abide in the Dharma: if one abides in the Dharma, this is to abide in the Dharma and not to seek the Dharma.

"One cannot see, hear, sense, or know the Dharma: if one practices seeing, hearing, sensing, and knowing, this is seeing, hearing, sensing, and knowing and not to seek the Dharma.

5. The Dharma is named the unconditioned: if one practices [within] the conditioned, this is to seek the conditioned and not to seek the Dharma.

"Therefore, Śāriputra, if one seeks the Dharma one should be without seeking regarding all the *dharmas*."

When he spoke these words, five hundred gods attained purity of the Dharma eye with regard to the *dharmas*.

6. At this time the Elder Vimalakīrti asked Mañjuśrī, "Sir, in your wanderings throughout the immeasurable ten million *koṭi*s of incalculable numbers of [Buddha] countries, which Buddha land has lion seats made with the best and most wondrous qualities?"

546b

Mañjuśrī said, "Retired scholar, in the east, as many countries away as there are grains of sand in thirty-six Ganges Rivers, there is a world-system called Characteristic of Sumeru. Its Buddha is called Sumeru Lamp King, who is manifest [in that world] at present. That Buddha's body is eighty-four thousand *yojana*s tall. His lion seat is eighty-four thousand *yojana*s high and paramount in ornamentation."

7. At this the Elder Vimalakīrti manifested the power of numinous penetration, and immediately that Buddha dispatched thirty-two thousand lion seats, tall, wide, and pure in ornamentation, which arrived in Vimalakīrti's room. This was something the bodhisattvas, great disciples, Indras, Brahmās, and four heavenly kings had never seen before.

The breadth of the room entirely accommodated the thirty-two thousand lion seats with no obstruction. Nor was there any deformation of the city of Vaiśālī, Jambudvīpa, or all the worlds of four continents. All appeared just as before.

8. At this time Vimalakīrti said to Mañjuśrī, "Take a lion seat and sit there along with the bodhisattvas and superior ones. You should adjust [the size of] your body to match the image of the seat."

Those bodhisattvas who had attained the numinous penetrations immediately transformed themselves to become forty-two thousand *yojana*s [tall] and sat on the lion seats. But none of the beginner bodhisattvas and great disciples were able to ascend [the seats].

At that time Vimalakīrti said to Śāriputra, "Take a lion seat."

Śāriputra said, "Retired scholar, this seat is [so] huge I am unable to ascend it."

Vimalakīrti said, "O Śāriputra, after you have worshiped Sumeru Lamp King Tathāgata you will be able to sit there."

Then the beginner bodhisattvas and great disciples worshiped Sumeru Lamp King Tathāgata and were immediately able to sit on the lion seats.

9. Śāriputra said, "Retired scholar, this is unprecedented! Such a small room has accommodated these huge seats, and there is no hindrance in the city of Vaiśālī, nor is there any distortion in the villages and towns of Jambudvīpa, nor in all the worlds of four continents, nor in the palaces of the gods, dragon kings, and demonic spirits."

10. Vimalakīrti said, "O Śāriputra, the Buddhas and bodhisattvas have an emancipation called 'inconceivable.' For a bodhisattva residing in this emancipation, the vastness of [Mount] Sumeru can be placed within a mustard seed without [either of them] increasing or decreasing in size. Sumeru, king of mountains, will remain in appearance as before, and the gods of the [heavens of the four heavenly kings and the Trayastriṃśa [Heaven] will not sense or know their own entry [into the mustard seed]. Only those one is trying to save will see Sumeru enter into the mustard seed. This is called abiding in the teaching of inconceivable emancipation.

11. "Also, [a bodhisattva] may cause the waters of the four great oceans to enter into a single pore.

546c

"[The bodhisattva does so] without discomforting the fish, turtles, tortoises, crocodiles, and [other] aquatic life forms, and the fundamental characteristics of those great oceans [remain] as before. The dragons, demonic spirits, and *asura*s do not realize that they have entered [into the single pore]. At this, the sentient beings [just mentioned] are not discomforted.

12. "Furthermore, Śāriputra, a bodhisattva residing in inconceivable emancipation who eradicates grasping of the great trimegachiliocosm does so just like a potter grasping a wheel in his right palm: were he to throw it past world-systems as numerous as the grains of sand in the Ganges River, the sentient beings within [that great trimegachiliocosm] would be unaware of where they had gone. Also, when it returns to its original location, none of them would have any conception of having gone and returned, and the fundamental characteristics of this world-system would be as before.

13. "Furthermore, Śāriputra, if there are sentient beings who can be saved through their desire for longevity, a bodhisattva will extend seven days into an entire *kalpa* and cause those sentient beings to consider it a *kalpa*. If there are sentient beings who can be saved through their desire for brevity of lifespan, a bodhisattva will compress an entire *kalpa* into seven days and cause those sentient beings to consider it [only] seven days.

14. "Furthermore, Śāriputra, a bodhisattva who resides in inconceivable emancipation can assemble the ornaments of all the Buddha lands in a single country to manifest them to sentient beings.

"Furthermore, a bodhisattva can take the sentient beings of a Buddha land in the right palm and fly to all ten directions, showing them everything, without moving from the original location.

"Furthermore, Śāriputra, a bodhisattva can make visible in a single pore all the articles offered to the Buddhas by [all] the sentient beings throughout the ten directions. Also, he can make visible all the suns, moons, and constellations of the countries of the ten directions.

"Furthermore, Śāriputra, a bodhisattva can without physical harm inhale through the mouth all the winds of the worlds in the ten directions, and the trees outside [the bodhisattva] will not be damaged [by the winds].

15. "Also, during the *kalpa*-ending conflagration of the world-systems of the ten directions, he can take all the fires within his abdomen, and though the fires will be as before he will not be harmed.

"Also, passing beyond Buddha world-systems in the lower direction more numerous than the sands of the Ganges River, he can take a single Buddha land and lift it up in the upper direction, passing beyond world-systems more numerous than the sands of the Ganges River. Like holding a needle or a thorn, he is not inconvenienced [at all by doing so].

16. "Also, Śāriputra, a bodhisattva who resides in inconceivable emancipation is able to use the numinous penetrations to manifest the body of a Buddha, or to manifest the body of a *pratyeka-buddha,* or to manifest the body of a *śrāvaka,* or to manifest the body of an Indra, or to manifest the body of a Brahmā king, or to manifest the body of a world lord (i.e., heavenly king), or to manifest the body of a universal ruler.

17. "Also, [a bodhisattva can take] all the sounds in the world-systems of the ten directions, high, medium, and low, and can

change them into the sounds (i.e., voices) of the Buddha, playing the sounds of impermanence, suffering, emptiness, and no-self, with all the various Dharmas explained by the Buddhas of the ten directions within those sounds, to be heard everywhere.

18. " Śāriputra, I have now briefly explained the power of the bodhisattva's inconceivable emancipation. If I were to explain it extensively a *kalpa* would be exhausted without completing it!"

19. Then Mahākāśyapa, hearing the teaching of the bodhisattva's inconceivable emancipation, exclaimed that it was unprecedented and said to Śāriputra, "It is as if someone displayed to a blind person all the colors and forms he cannot see. In the same fashion, when all the *śrāvaka*s hear this teaching of the inconceivable emancipation, they are not able to comprehend it. When the wise hear it, who among them would not generate the intention to achieve *anuttarā samyaksaṃbodhi*?

"How is it that we have long cut off our capacity [for understanding]? With regard to this Mahayana we are like destroyed seeds. When all the *śrāvaka*s hear this teaching of the inconceivable emancipation, they should all scream out a cry to shake the trimegachiliocosm. All the bodhisattvas should accept this Dharma with great joy.

"If there are bodhisattvas who devoutly understand this teaching of inconceivable emancipation, all the congregations of Māras will be unable to do anything to them." When Mahākāśyapa spoke these words, thirty-two thousand gods all generated the intention to achieve *anuttarā samyaksaṃbodhi*.

20. At that time Vimalakīrti said to Mahākāśyapa, "Sir, the majority of those acting as Māra kings in the incalculable *asaṃkhyeya*s of world-systems are bodhisattvas residing in the inconceivable emancipation. They manifest themselves as Māra kings through the power of skillful means, to teach sentient beings.

"Also, Kāśyapa, as to the immeasurable bodhisattvas of the ten directions, there may be people who beg them for a hand, foot, ear, nose, head, eye, marrow, brain matter, blood, flesh, skin, bone, village, town, wife and sons, slave, elephant, horse, vehicle, gold, silver, lapis lazuli, sapphire, agate, coral, emerald, pearl, conch shell, clothing, or food.

"Beggars such as these are usually bodhisattvas residing in the inconceivable emancipation, who use the power of skillful means to go test [the bodhisattvas] and make them resolute. Why? Bodhisattvas who reside in the inconceivable emancipation possess the power of awesome virtue and therefore manifest the practice of pressuring, showing sentient beings difficulties such as these. Ordinary people are inferior and lack energy, and they are unable to pressure bodhisattvas in this way. It is like the kick of a dragon or elephant, which is not something a donkey could withstand.

"This is called the 'gate of wisdom and skillful means of bodhisattvas residing in the inconceivable emancipation.'"

Chapter VII

Viewing Sentient Beings

1. At this point Mañjuśrī asked Vimalakīrti, "How should the bodhisattva view sentient beings?"

Vimalakīrti said,

i) "As if he were a magician seeing a conjured person, so should a bodhisattva view sentient beings.

ii) "Like a wise person seeing the moon in water,

iii) like seeing the image of a face in a mirror,

iv) like a mirage when it is hot,

v) like the echo of a shout,

vi) like clouds in the sky,

vii) like water collecting into foam,

viii) like bubbles upon water,

ix) like the firmness of the banana tree,

x) like the prolonged abiding of lightning,

xi) like a fifth element,

xii) like a sixth *skandha,*

xiii) like a seventh sense,

xiv) like a thirteenth entrance (*āyatana*),

xv) like a nineteenth realm (*dhātu*)—so should a bodhisattva view sentient beings.

xvi) "Like form in the formless realm,

xvii) like a seedling emerging from burned grain,

xviii) like a stream-enterer's mistaken view of the body,

xix) like a non-returner's (*anāgāmin*) entrance into a womb,

xx) like an arhat's three poisons,

xxi) like a bodhisattva who has achieved forbearance breaking the prohibition against anger,

xxii) like a Buddha's latent influences of the afflictions,

xxiii) like a blind man seeing forms,

xxiv) like the inhalation and exhalation of someone who has entered the concentration of extinction,

xxv) like the tracks of birds in the sky, like the child of a barren woman,

xxvi) like a conjured person generating the afflictions, like waking up in a dream,

xxvii) like one who has entered nirvana being reborn, like fire without smoke—so should a bodhisattva view sentient beings."

2. Mañjuśrī said, "If a bodhisattva views sentient beings in this fashion, how should he practice sympathy?"

Vimalakīrti said, "The bodhisattva who views [sentient beings] in this fashion should think to himself, 'I should explain the Dharma for sentient beings in this fashion, and this will constitute true sympathy.

"'I should practice the sympathy of extinction, because of the absence of anything generated;

"'[I should] practice the sympathy of no-heat, because of the absence of the afflictions;

"'[I should] practice the sympathy of sameness, because of the sameness of the three periods of time;

"'[I should] practice the sympathy of nondisputation, because of the absence of generation;

"'[I should] practice the sympathy of nonduality, because of the nonconjunction of interior and exterior;

"'[I should] practice the sympathy of nondestruction, because of the ultimate exhaustion [of the characteristics of sympathy];

"'[I should] practice the sympathy of resoluteness, because of indestructibility; practice the sympathy of purity, because of the essential purity of the *dharmas*;

"'[I should] practice the sympathy of no extremes, because of its being like space; practice the sympathy of an arhat, because of the destruction of the "bandits" of the fetters;

"'[I should] practice the sympathy of a bodhisattva, because of the pacification of sentient beings; practice the sympathy of a Tathāgata, because of attainment of the characteristic of "thusness";

"'[I should] practice the sympathy of a Buddha, because of the enlightenment of sentient beings; practice the sympathy of the naturally [accomplished sage], because of the imperceptibility of causes;

"'[I should] practice the sympathy of *bodhi,* because of the sameness of the single taste;

"'[I should] practice the sympathy of inequivalence, because of the eradication of the affections;

"'[I should] practice the sympathy of great compassion, because of guiding [sentient beings] by means of the Mahayana;

"'[I should] practice the sympathy of nonrevulsion, because of the contemplation of emptiness and no-self;

"'[I should] practice the sympathy of the charity of Dharma, because of the absence of regrets;

"'[I should] practice the sympathy of morality, because of converting the transgressors; practice the sympathy of forbearance, because of protecting others and self;

"'[I should] practice the sympathy of exertion, because of carrying the burden for sentient beings;

"'[I should] practice the sympathy of concentration, because of not experiencing the flavors [of desire];

"'[I should] practice the sympathy of wisdom, because of the absence of any time of non-understanding;

"'[I should] practice the sympathy of skillful means, because of the manifestation of all [teaching methods];

"'[I should] practice the sympathy of non-hiding, because of the purity of sincerity;

"'[I should] practice the sympathy of the profound mind,   547c
because of the absence of heterogeneous practices;

"'[I should] practice the sympathy of the non-crazed, because of not using false conventions;

"'[I should] practice the sympathy of peace and joy, because of causing [beings] to attain the joy of Buddhahood—thus is the sympathy of the bodhisattva.'"

3. Mañjuśrī asked further, "What is compassion?"

[Vimalakīrti] answered, "The merits achieved by the bodhisattva are entirely shared with all sentient beings."

[Question:] "What is joy?"

Answer: "If there is benefit, then one rejoices without regret."

[Question:] "What is forsaking?"

Answer: "The blessings generated are without expectation."

4. Mañjuśrī also asked, "For the bodhisattva who fears samsara, what should be his reliance?"

Vimalakīrti said, "A bodhisattva who fears samsara should rely on the power of the Tathāgata's merit."

Mañjuśrī also asked, "The bodhisattva who wishes to rely on the power of the Tathāgata's merit—in what should he abide?"

Answer: "The bodhisattva who wishes to rely on the power of the Tathāgata's merit should abide in saving all sentient beings."

5. [Mañjuśrī] also asked, "If one wishes to save sentient beings, what should be eradicated?"

Answer: "If one wishes to save sentient beings, the afflictions should be eradicated."

[Mañjuśrī] also asked, "If one wishes to eradicate the afflictions, what should one practice?"

Answer: "One should practice correct mindfulness."

[Mañjuśrī] also asked, "How does one practice correct mindfulness?"

Answer: "One should practice nongeneration and nonextinction."

[Mañjuśrī] also asked, "What *dharmas* are nongenerated and what *dharmas* are nonextinguished?"

Answer: "The not-good are [to be] nongenerated, and the good *dharmas* are [to be] nonextinguished."

[Mañjuśrī] also asked, "What is the fundamental basis of good and bad [*dharmas*]?"

Answer: "The body is their fundamental basis."

[Mañjuśrī] also asked, "What is the fundamental basis of the body?"

Answer: "Desire is its fundamental basis."

[Mañjuśrī] also asked, "What is the fundamental basis of desire?"

Answer: "False discrimination is its fundamental basis."

6. [Mañjuśrī] also asked, "What is the fundamental basis of false discrimination?"

Answer: "Confused conception is its fundamental basis."

[Mañjuśrī] also asked, "What is the fundamental basis of confused conception?"

Answer: "The nonabiding is its fundamental basis."

[Mañjuśrī] also asked, "What is the fundamental basis of nonabiding?"

Answer: "Nonabiding is without any fundamental [basis]. Mañjuśrī, all *dharmas* are established on the fundamental [basis] of nonabiding."

7. At the time, there was a goddess in Vimalakīrti's room who, upon seeing the great men listening to the Dharma being explained, made herself visible and scattered heavenly flowers over the bodhisattvas and great disciples. When the flowers reached the bodhisattvas they all immediately fell off, but when they reached the great disciples they adhered and did not fall off. Even using all their numinous powers, the disciples were unable to remove the flowers.

8. At that time, the goddess asked Śāriputra, "Why would you remove the flowers?"

[Śāriputra] answered, "These flowers are contrary to the Dharma, so I would remove them."

The goddess said, "Do not say that these flowers are contrary to the Dharma! Why? These flowers are without discrimination. Sir, it is you who are generating discriminative thoughts. If one who has left home in the Buddha-Dharma has discrimination, this is contrary to the Dharma; if such a one is without discrimination, this is in accord with the Dharma. 548a

143

"Look at the bodhisattvas, to whom the flowers do not adhere—this is because they have eradicated all discriminative thoughts.

"For example, when a person is afraid, non-human [beings] are able to control him. Thus, since the disciples fear samsara, then forms, sounds, smells, tastes, and tangibles control you. None of the five desires can affect those who have transcended fear.

"It is only because the latent influences [of your afflictions] are not yet exhausted that the flowers stick to your bodies.

"For those in whom the latent influences are exhausted, the flowers do not stick."

9. Śāriputra said, "Have you stayed in this room long?"

Answer: "I have stayed in this room as long as you have been emancipated."

Śāriputra said, "How long have you stayed here?"

The goddess said, "How long has it been since your emancipation?"

Śāriputra was silent and did not answer.

The goddess said, "What is your great wisdom that you remain silent?"

Answer: "Emancipation is not to be spoken of, and so I did not know what to say."

The goddess said, "Speech and words are entirely the characteristics of emancipation. Why?

"Emancipation is neither internal, nor external, nor intermediate. Words are also neither internal, nor external, nor intermediate. Therefore, Śāriputra, the explanation of emancipation does not transcend words. Why?

"All *dharmas* have the characteristic of emancipation."

Śāriputra said, "Is it not also that emancipation is the transcendence of licentiousness, anger, and stupidity?"

The goddess said, "On behalf of the self-conceited, the Buddha explained that emancipation is the transcendence of licentiousness, anger, and stupidity. If one is not self-conceited, the Buddha explains that licentiousness, anger, and stupidity are emancipation."

10. Śāriputra said, "Excellent, excellent! O goddess, what attainment do you have, and through what realization do you have eloquence such as this?"

The goddess said, "It is because I am without attainment and without realization that my eloquence is like this. Why? If one had attainment and realization, this would be to be self-conceited with regard to the Buddha-Dharma."

11. Śāriputra asked the goddess, "Which of the three vehicles do you seek?"

The goddess said, "Since I convert sentient beings with the *śrāvaka* Dharma I am a *śrāvaka*. Since I convert sentient beings with the Dharma of causality I am a *pratyekabuddha*. Since I convert sentient beings with the Dharma of great compassion, I am a Mahayanist.

12. "Śāriputra, just as a person who has entered a *campaka* forest can smell only *campaka* and no other smells, thus it is if you enter this room—you can smell only the fragrance of the Buddha's merit and do not delight in smelling the fragrance of the merit of *śrāvaka*s and *pratyekabuddha*s.

"Śāriputra, those Indras, Brahmās, four heavenly kings, and the gods, dragons, and spirits who enter this room all hear this Superior One (i.e., Vimalakīrti) explain the correct Dharma, and they all leave delighting [only] in the fragrance of the Buddha's merit and generating the intention [to achieve *anuttarā samyak-* 548b *saṃbodhi*].

"Śāriputra, I have stayed in this room twelve years. From the beginning I have not heard the Dharma of *śrāvaka* and *pratyeka-buddha;* I have only heard the Buddhas' inconceivable Dharma of the bodhisattvas' great sympathy and great compassion.

13. "Śāriputra, this room constantly manifests eight unprecedentedly rare *dharma*s. What are these eight?

i) "This room is always illuminated with golden light, with no variation day or night. It is not bright due to the illumination of sun and moon. This is the first unprecedentedly rare *dharma*.

ii) "Those who enter this room are not afflicted by the defilements. This is the second unprecedentedly rare *dharma*.

iii) "This room always has Indras, Brahmās, the four heavenly kings, and bodhisattvas from other regions who arrive and gather without interruption. This is the third unprecedentedly rare *dharma*.

iv) "In this room there is constant explanation of the six perfections and the nonretrogressive Dharma. This is the fourth unprecedentedly rare *dharma*.

v) "This room always produces the gods' supreme string music, which generates the sound of the teaching of the immeasurable Dharma. This is the fifth unprecedentedly rare *dharma*.

vi) "This room has four great storehouses filled with the many jewels, which are given to the destitute and used to save the poor without limit. This is the sixth unprecedentedly rare *dharma*.

vii) "To this room Śākyamuni Buddha, Amitābha Buddha, Akṣobhya Buddha, Jewel Virtue Buddha, Jewel Mirage Buddha, Jewel Moon Buddha, Jewel Ornament Buddha, Difficult to Overcome Buddha, Lion's Echo Buddha, and Achievement of All Benefits Buddha, and the immeasurable Buddhas of the ten directions such as these all come when the Superior One is mindful of them; and they extensively explain to him the Buddhas' secret Dharma storehouse and, having explained it, then return [to their own worlds]. This is the seventh unprecedentedly rare *dharma*.

viii) "In this room appear all the ornamented palaces of the gods and the pure lands of the Buddhas. This is the eighth unprecedentedly rare *dharma*.

"Śāriputra, this room always manifests the eight unprecedentedly rare *dharma*s. Who could see these inconceivable things and still take pleasure in the *śrāvaka* Dharma?"

14. Śāriputra said, "Why do you not transform your female body?"

The goddess said, "For the past twelve years I have sought the characteristic of being female and have comprehended it to be unattainable (i.e., imperceptible). Why should I transform it? It is as if a magician has created a conjured female. If someone asked her, 'Why do you not transform your female body?' would that person's question be proper or not?"

Śāriputra said, "It would not. An indeterminate characteristic that has been conjured—why should it be transformed?"

The goddess said, "All *dharmas* are also like this, in being without determinate characteristics. So why do you ask, 'Why do you not transform your female body?'"

15. Then the goddess used the power of numinous penetration and changed Śāriputra's body to be like that of a goddess, and she transformed her own body to be like Śāriputra. She then asked, "Why do you not transform this female body?"

Śāriputra, in the goddess's form, answered, "I do not know how   548c
you transformed me now into this female body."

The goddess said, "Śāriputra, if you were able to transform this female body, then all females would also be able to transform themselves. Just as Śāriputra is not female but is manifesting a female body, so are all females likewise. Although they manifest female bodies, they are not female.

"Therefore, the Buddha has explained that all *dharmas* are neither male nor female."

At this point the goddess withdrew her numinous power, and Śāriputra's body returned to as it was before.

The goddess asked Śāriputra, "Now where does the characteristic of form of the female body occur?"

Śāriputra said, "The characteristic of form of the female body is without occurrence and without non-occurrence."

The goddess said, "All the *dharmas* are also likewise, in being without occurrence and without non-occurrence. This 'without occurrence and without non-occurrence' is as the Buddhas have explained."

16. Śāriputra asked the goddess, "When you die here, where will you be reborn?"

The goddess said, "Wherever the Buddha's [activity of] conversion is born (i.e., generated), likewise will I be born."

[Śāriputra] said, "Where the Buddha's [activity of] conversion is generated is not [a place] of death and birth."

The goddess said, "Sentient beings are likewise without death and birth."

Śāriputra asked the goddess, "How long will it be until you attain *anuttarā samyaksambodhi*?"

The goddess said, "When you are reborn as an [unenlightened] ordinary person, I will achieve *anuttarā samyaksambodhi*."

Śāriputra said, "For me to be an ordinary person—this will never happen!"

The goddess said, "My attaining of *anuttarā samyaksam-bodhi*—this too will never happen. Why? *Bodhi* is without any locus of abiding. Therefore there is no one who attains it."

Śāriputra said, "The Buddhas who attain *anuttarā samyak-sambodhi,* including those who have attained it and those who will attain it, are as numerous as the sands of the Ganges River. What about all of them?"

The goddess said, "It is entirely through conventional words and numbers that one talks of the existence of the three periods of time. It is not that there is past, future, and present in *bodhi*!"

The goddess said, "Śāriputra, have you attained arhatship?"

[Śāriputra] said, "There is no attainment, and so have I attained it."

The goddess said, "The Buddhas and bodhisattvas are also like this. There is no attainment, and so have they attained [*anuttarā samyaksambodhi*]."

17. At this time Vimalakīrti said to Śāriputra, "The goddess has already served ninety-two *koṭis* of Buddhas. She is able to disport in the numinous penetrations of the bodhisattva, her vows are complete, she has attained forbearance of the nonarising of *dharma*s, and she abides in nonretrogression. By virtue of her original vows she is able to manifest the teaching of sentient beings as she wishes."

Chapter VIII

The Path of Buddhahood

1. Mañjuśrī then asked Vimalakīrti, "How should the bodhisattva penetrate the path of Buddhahood?"

Vimalakīrti said, "If a bodhisattva traverses the unacceptable paths, this is to penetrate the path of Buddhahood."

[Mañjuśrī] also asked, "How does the bodhisattva traverse the unacceptable paths?"

[Vimalakīrti] answered, "The bodhisattva practices the five [deeds of] interminable [retribution] without becoming distraught.

"He goes to the hells without the defilements of transgression; goes among the animals without the errors of ignorance, conceit, and so on.

"He goes among the hungry ghosts replete in merit; traverses the paths of the form and formless realms without considering himself superior.

"He manifests acting out of desire but transcends the defiled attachments; manifests acting out of anger at sentient beings but is without aversion.

"He manifests acting out of stupidity but uses wisdom to control his mind.

"He manifests acting out of lust but forsakes both internal and external and does not begrudge his own life; manifests the practicing of moral infractions but peacefully resides in the pure precepts, even unto harboring great fear about even minor transgressions; manifests acting out of anger but is always sympathetically forbearant; manifests acting out of laziness, yet vigorously cultivates merit; manifests acting out of a disturbed mind, yet is always mindfully concentrated; manifests acting out of stupidity, yet penetrates both mundane and supramundane wisdom.

149

"He manifests the practicing of flattery and deception, yet uses good skillful means to accord with the meanings found in the sutras; manifests acting out of conceit, yet is like a bridge for sentient beings.

"He manifests acting out of the afflictions, yet is always pure in mind; manifests becoming a Māra, yet accords with the wisdom of the Buddha and follows no other teaching; manifests becoming a *śrāvaka*, yet for sentient beings explains Dharmas they have not heard before; manifests becoming a *pratyekabuddha,* yet accomplishes great compassion to teach sentient beings; manifests becoming destitute, yet has the unlimited merit of the 'hand of treasures'; manifests becoming maimed through criminal punishment, yet adorns himself with all the [thirty-two primary] characteristics and [eighty subsidiary] marks; manifests becoming low-born, yet is [actually] born within the Buddha's lineage and replete in its various merits; manifests becoming feeble and ugly, yet attains the body of a Nārāyaṇa, which all sentient beings enjoy seeing.

"He manifests becoming old and sick, yet always eradicates the roots of illness and transcends the fear of death.

"He manifests having the material requisites, yet always views [the world as] impermanent and is truly without desire; manifests having wife, concubines, and mistresses, yet always distantly transcends the muddy filth of the five desires; manifests dumbness (i.e., muteness), yet accomplishes eloquence and unfailing *dhāraṇī*s.

"He manifests becoming a 'false ford' (i.e., a heretic), yet uses the correct ford to 'cross over' sentient beings [to salvation].

"He manifests entering all the destinies, yet eradicates their causes and conditions; and manifests nirvana, yet does not eradicate samsara.

"Mañjuśrī, if a bodhisattva can traverse the unacceptable paths in this way, this is to penetrate the path of Buddhahood."

2. At this Vimalakīrti asked Mañjuśrī, "What is the seed of the Tathāgata?"

Mañjuśrī said, "The possession of a body constitutes this seed. Ignorance and affection constitute this seed. Lust, anger, and stupidity constitute this seed. The four confusions constitute this seed.

549b

The five hindrances constitute this seed. The six entrances (*āyatana*s) constitute this seed. The seven loci of consciousness constitute this seed. The eight heterodox *dharma*s and nine loci of affliction constitute this seed. The ten evil actions constitute this seed. In essence, the sixty-two mistaken views and all the afflictions constitute this seed."

3. [Vimalakīrti] said, "Why is this?"

[Mañjuśrī] answered, "Anyone who sees the unconditioned and enters the primary status [of Hinayana enlightenment] will be unable to generate the intention to achieve *anuttarā samyaksaṃbodhi*.

"It is just as lotus flowers do not grow on dry land on the high plateau—these flowers grow in the muddy filth of the lowly marshes. Thus one who sees the unconditioned *dharma*s and enters the primary status will never be able to generate the *dharma*s of a Buddha. It is only within the mud of the afflictions that sentient beings give rise to the *dharma*s of a Buddha.

"Or again, it is like planting a seed in space, where it would never grow—only in nightsoil-enriched earth can it flourish. In this way, one who enters the unconditioned primary status will not be able to generate the *dharma*s of a Buddha.

"It is only when one generates a view of self as great as Mount Sumeru that one is able to generate the intention to achieve *anuttarā samyaksaṃbodhi* and generate the *dharma*s of a Buddha.

"Therefore, you should understand that all the afflictions constitute the seed of the Tathāgata. It is like not being able to attain the priceless jewel-pearl without entering the ocean. Therefore, if one does not enter the great sea of the afflictions, one will not be able to attain the jewel of omniscience."

4. At this time Mahākāśyapa exclaimed, "Excellent, excellent, Mañjuśrī! It is well that you have spoken thus; truly, it is as you have said! The field of the sensory troubles constitutes the seed of the Tathāgata.

"We [disciples] are now unable to bear generating the intention to achieve *anuttarā samyaksaṃbodhi*. It will only be after [we have committed] the transgressions [leading to] the five interminable [hells] that we will be able to generate that intention and generate the *dharma*s of a Buddha. [As we are] now we will never be able to generate it.

5. "It is like a man whose sense organs are destroyed being unable to benefit from the five desires. Likewise, *śrāvaka*s who have eradicated the fetters are unable to benefit from the *dharma*s of a Buddha and will never vow [to achieve Buddhahood].

6. "Therefore, Mañjuśrī, ordinary people can respond to the *dharma*s of a Buddha, but *śrāvaka*s cannot. Why? When an ordinary person hears the Buddha-Dharma he is able to generate the intention to achieve unsurpassable enlightenment and not eradicate the Three Jewels. Even if *śrāvaka*s spend their whole lives hearing about the *dharma*s of a Buddha, [including the ten] powers, [the four] fearlessnesses, [and the other] unique [*dharma*s of a Buddha], they will never be able to generate the intention to achieve unsurpassable enlightenment!"

7. At that time there was a bodhisattva in the assembly named Universally Manifests the Form Body. He asked Vimalakīrti,

"O retired scholar, who are your parents, wife and sons, relatives, subordinates, servants, and friends? Where are your slaves, servants, elephants, horses, and vehicles?"

549c

At this, Vimalakīrti replied in verse:

1. The perfection of wisdom is the bodhisattva's mother;
   Skillful means is his father.
   All the assembly of guides
   Without exception are the causes of his birth.

2. Joy in the Dharma is his wife,
   And the mind of sympathy and compassion his daughters.
   The mind of goodness and sincerity is his sons,
   And ultimate emptiness and serenity his home.

3. His congregation of disciples is the sensory troubles,
   Which he converts as he wishes.
   The factors of enlightenment are his good friends,
   On whom he depends to achieve correct enlightenment.

4. The *dharma*s of the perfections are his companions,
   And the four types of attraction his dancing girls,
   Who sing the words of Dharma
   And thereby create their music.

5. In the garden of *dhāraṇī*
   And the grove of the flawless Dharma,
   Is the pure and wonderful flower of the intention for
       enlightenment
   And the fruit of wisdom and emancipation.

6. The pool of the eight emancipations
   Is filled with the peaceful waters of concentration.
   Scattering the flowers of the seven purities,
   Here bathe the undefiled persons.

7. His elephants and horses are the five penetrations
       that race,
   And the Mahayana is his chariot.
   Control is through singlemindedness,
   So he wanders the roads of the eightfold correct [paths].

8. With the [thirty-two primary] characteristics replete to
       ornament his form,
   And the host of [eighty subsidiary] marks to decorate his
       bodies,
   Shame is his upper garment,
   And the profound mind his flowered necklace.

9. His wealth is the seven treasures [of the Dharma],
   Which he bestows in teaching so that [beings] will flourish.
   He practices according to [the Buddha's] explanation
   And rededicates [the ensuing merit] for great benefit.

10. The four *dhyāna*s are his seat,
    From which his pure livelihood is generated.
    Erudition increases his wisdom
    And becomes the sound of his own enlightenment.

11. His food is the sweet dew of the Dharma,
    And his drink the flavor of emancipation.
    With the pure mind does he bathe,
    Using the categories of the precepts as his incense
      powder.

12. Demolishing the bandits of the afflictions,
    He is courageous and invincible.
    Subjugating the four types of Māras,
    The banner of his victory is erected at the place of
      enlightenment.

13. Although he understands there is no generation
      and no extinction,
    He is born so as to manifest [the Dharma] to others.
    He manifests all the countries,
    With none invisible, as [plain as] the sun.

14. He makes offerings to the immeasurable *koṭi*s
    Of Tathāgatas throughout the ten directions,
    Without having any thought of discriminating
    Between the Buddhas and himself.

15. Although he understands that the Buddha lands
    And sentient beings are empty,
    He always practices purifying his land,
    Teaching the hosts of beings.

16. The various categories of sentient beings—
    Their forms, sounds, and deportments—
    The bodhisattva with the power of fearlessness
    Can simultaneously manifest them all.

17. Recognizing the affairs of the host of Māras,
    And while seeming to go along with their activities,
    He uses wisdom and good skillful means,
    So that he can manifest anything he wishes.

550a

18. He may manifest old age, illness, and death
    To accomplish [the liberation of] the hosts of beings.
    Comprehending that [all things] are like phantasma-
        gorical transformations,
    His penetration is without hindrance.

19. He may manifest the *kalpa*-ending conflagration,
    In which heaven and earth are entirely incinerated.
    To the hosts of people who have the conception of
        permanence,
    He illuminates [the truth] so that they understand
        impermanence.

20. Innumerable *koṭi*s of sentient beings
    All come to request the bodhisattva's [assistance].
    He simultaneously goes to their homes
    And converts them so that they turn toward the path of
        Buddhahood.

21. The magical arts prohibited in the scriptures,
    The various skills and arts—
    He manifests the performance of all these things
    To benefit the hosts of beings.

22. In all the religious teachings of this world
    Does he leave home [to dedicate himself],
    Thereby to release people from their delusions,
    So they will not fall into heterodox views.

23. He may become the god of the sun or moon,
    A Brahmā king, or a world lord,
    And at times he may become earth or water,
    Or again wind or fire.

24. When there are epidemics in the middle of a *kalpa*
    He manifests himself as medicinal plants.
    If someone takes [these herbs],
    They eradicate illness and eliminate the host of poisons.

25. When there are famines in the middle of a *kalpa*
    He manifests himself as food and drink,
    First saving the hungry and thirsty,
    And then speaking of the Dharma to people.

26. When armed soldiers appear in the middle of a *kalpa*
    He generates sympathy for them.
    He converts the sentient beings,
    Causing them to abide in noncontention.

27. If there are great armies
    Facing each other with equal strength,
    The bodhisattva manifests his awesome power,
    And, subjugating them, imposes peace.

28. In all the countries,
    Wherever there are hells
    Does he go to save [the beings there]
    From their sufferings.

29. In all the countries,
    Wherever animals devour one another,
    He always manifests being born there
    To provide benefit for them there.

30. He manifests experiencing the five desires
    And also manifests the practice of *dhyāna*,
    Making Māra distressed
    At being unable to take control.

31. For a lotus flower to be born in the midst of fire
    Can certainly be called rare!
    To practice *dhyāna* within the desires—
    This is just as rare.

32. He may manifest himself as a prostitute,
    Enticing those who enjoy sensuality.
    First enticing them with desire,
    And later causing them to enter the wisdom of the Buddha.

33. He may become a village master,
    Or become a merchant guide,
    National teacher, great minister—
    In order to benefit sentient beings.

34. For the destitute
    He manifests inexhaustible treasuries,
    Thereby exhorting and guiding them,
    Causing them to generate the intention to achieve
        enlightenment.

35. For those who are selfish and conceited,
    He manifests himself as a great warrior,
    Decimating the pretensions [of sentient beings],
    And causing them to abide in the unsurpassable path.

36. The hosts of the fear-stricken
    He shields and comforts,
    First giving them fearlessness
    And then causing them to generate the intention to
        achieve enlightenment.

37. He may manifest the transcendence of licentious desire
    And become a transcendent of the five penetrations,
    Guiding the hosts of beings
    And making them abide in morality, forbearance,
        and sympathy.

38. Seeing those who should be served,
    He manifests himself as a servant.
    Taking joy in the affirmation of one's intention,
    [Those to be honored] generate the intention to achieve
        enlightenment.

39. In accordance with the needs of others,
    He causes them to enter into the path of Buddhahood.
    Using the power of good skillful means
    He provides sufficiency to all.

40. Thus are the paths immeasurable
    Which he traverses without restriction.
    His wisdom is without limit
    In saving the innumerable hosts [of beings].

41. Even if we had all the Buddhas
    Throughout immeasurable *koṭi*s of *kalpa*s
    Praise his merits,
    They would not be able to do so completely.

42. Whoever hears the Dharma such as this
    And does not generate the intention to achieve *bodhi*—
    Excluding those who do not even seem human—
    Are ignorant fools.

Chapter IX

The Dharma Gate of Nonduality

1. At that time Vimalakīrti said to the congregation of bodhi- 550c
sattvas, "Sirs, how does the bodhisattva enter the Dharma gate of
nonduality? Each of you explain this as you wish."

Within the assembly was a bodhisattva named Autonomous
Dharma, who said, "Sirs, generation and extinction (i.e., samsara)
constitute a duality. Since the *dharma*s were fundamentally not
generated, now they are without extinction. To attain this [under-
standing is to achieve] forbearance of the nonarising of *dharma*s.
This is to enter the Dharma gate of nonduality."

2. Maintenance of Virtue Bodhisattva said, "The self and the
self's attributes constitute a duality. It is because of the existence
of the self that the self's attributes occur. If the self does not exist,
then there are no attributes of self. This is to enter the Dharma
gate of nonduality."

3. Unblinking Bodhisattva said, "Experience and nonexperience constitute a duality. If *dharma*s are not experienced, they
cannot be attained (i.e., are imperceptible). Because of unattainability, there is no grasping, no forsaking, no production, and no
activity. This is to enter the Dharma gate of nonduality."

4. Crown of Virtue Bodhisattva said, "Defilement and purity constitute a duality. If one sees the real nature of defilement, then there
is no characteristic of purity, and one accords with the extinction of
characteristics. This is to enter the Dharma gate of nonduality."

5. Excellent Constellation Bodhisattva said, "Motion and mindfulness constitute a duality. If there is motionlessness, there is no-
mindfulness. If there is no-mindfulness, there is no discrimination.
To penetrate this is to enter the Dharma gate of nonduality."

6. Excellent Eye Bodhisattva said, "The single characteristic and the non-characteristic constitute a duality. If one understands that the single characteristic is the non-characteristic, and does not grasp the non-characteristic but enters into universal sameness, this is to enter the Dharma gate of nonduality."

7. Wonderful Arm Bodhisattva said, "The aspirations of bodhisattvas and the aspirations of *śrāvaka*s constitute a duality. If one contemplates that the characteristics of mind (i.e., mental aspirations) are empty, like phantasmagorical transformations, there is no aspiration of bodhisattvas and no aspiration of *śrāvaka*s. This is to enter the Dharma gate of nonduality."

8. Puṣya Bodhisattva said, "What is good and what is not good constitute a duality. If one does not generate the good and what is not good, entering into and penetrating the limit of the non-characteristics, this is to enter the Dharma gate of nonduality."

9. Lion Bodhisattva said, "Transgression and blessing constitute a duality. If one penetrates the nature of transgression, then it is not different from blessings. Using the *vajra* wisdom to definitively comprehend this characteristic, and to be neither in bondage nor emancipated, is to enter the Dharma gate of nonduality."

10. Lion Mind Bodhisattva said, "To have flaws and to be flawless constitute a duality. If one can attain the equivalence of the *dharma*s, then one will not generate the conception of flaws and flawlessness. Being unattached to characteristics, but also not abiding in the absence of characteristics, is to enter the Dharma gate of nonduality."

11. Pure Emancipation Bodhisattva said, "The constructed and the unconstructed constitute a duality. If one transcends all categories, then the mind is like space. If one's wisdom is pure and without hindrance, this is to enter the Dharma gate of nonduality."

12. Nārāyaṇa Bodhisattva said, "The mundane and supramundane constitute a duality. The emptiness that is the nature of the mundane is the supramundane. Within these to neither enter nor exit, neither overflow nor disperse, is to enter the Dharma gate of nonduality."

13. Excellent Mind Bodhisattva said, "Samsara and nirvana constitute a duality. If one sees the nature of samsara, there is no samsara. To be without bondage and without emancipation, neither generating nor extinguished—to understand in this way is to enter the Dharma gate of nonduality."

14. Manifest Perception Bodhisattva said, "Exhaustible and inexhaustible constitute a duality. Whether the *dharmas* are ultimately exhaustible or inexhaustible, they are all [marked by] the characteristic of inexhaustibility. The characteristic of inexhaustibility is emptiness. Emptiness is without the characteristics of exhaustible and inexhaustible. To enter thus is to enter the Dharma gate of nonduality."

15. Universal Maintenance Bodhisattva said, "Self and no-self constitute a duality. Since even the self is unattainable, how could no-self be attainable? Those who see the real nature of the self will never again generate duality. This is to enter the Dharma gate of nonduality."

16. Thunder God Bodhisattva said, "Wisdom and ignorance constitute a duality. The real nature of ignorance is wisdom. Furthermore, wisdom cannot grasp and transcend all the categories [of reality]. To be universally same and nondual with respect to this is to enter the Dharma gate of nonduality."

17. Joyful Vision Bodhisattva said, "Form and the emptiness of form constitute a duality. Form is emptiness—it is not that form extinguishes emptiness but that the nature of form is of itself empty. Likewise are feeling, conception, process, and consciousness. Consciousness and emptiness are two. Consciousness is emptiness—it is not that consciousness extinguishes emptiness but that the nature of consciousness is of itself empty. To [abide] within and penetrate this is to enter the Dharma gate of nonduality."

18. Characteristic of Wisdom Bodhisattva said, "The differentiation of the four types [of elements] (i.e., earth, water, fire, and air) and the differentiation of the type of space constitute a duality. The nature of the four types [of elements] is the nature of emptiness. Given that the former and latter [types of elements]

are empty, the intermediate is also empty. To understand the natures of the types [of elements] in this way is to enter the Dharma gate of nonduality."

19. Wonderful Mind Bodhisattva said, "The eye and forms constitute a duality. If one understands that the nature of the eye is neither licentious, nor angry, nor stupid with regard to forms, this is called serene extinction. Likewise, the ear and sounds, the nose and smells, the tongue and tastes, the body and tangibles, and the mind and *dharmas* constitute dualities. If one understands that the nature of the mind is neither licentious, nor angry, nor stupid with regard to *dharmas*, this is called serene extinction. To abide peacefully within this is to enter the Dharma gate of nonduality."

20. Inexhaustible Mind Bodhisattva said, "Charity and the rededication [of the merit of charity] to omniscience constitute a duality. The nature of charity is the nature of the rededication to omniscience. Likewise, morality, forbearance, exertion, meditation, and wisdom constitute dualities with the rededication to omniscience. The nature of wisdom is the nature of the rededication to omniscience. To enter the single characteristic with respect to this is to enter the Dharma gate of nonduality."

21. Profound Wisdom Bodhisattva said, "[The three emancipations of] emptiness, signlessness, and wishlessness constitute dualities. The empty is the signless, and the signless is the wishless. If [one achieves] the empty, the signless, and the wishless, then there is no mind, thought, or consciousness. In this single gate of emancipation are the three gates of emancipation. This is to enter the Dharma gate of nonduality."

22. Serene Capacity Bodhisattva said, "Buddha, Dharma, and Sangha constitute dualities. The Buddha is the Dharma, and the Dharma is the Sangha. These Three Jewels all [have] the characteristic of the unconditioned and are equivalent to space, and all *dharmas* are also likewise. To be able to practice accordingly is to enter the Dharma gate of nonduality."

23. Unhindered Mind Bodhisattva said, "The body and the extinction of the body constitute a duality. The body is identical

to the extinction of the body. Why? Those who see the real characteristic of the body do not generate seeing the body and seeing the extinction of the body. Body and the extinction of the body are without duality and cannot be differentiated (lit., "without discrimination"). To neither be surprised or afraid with respect to this is to enter the Dharma gate of nonduality."

24. Superior Excellence Bodhisattva said, "The good [actions] of body, speech, and mind constitute dualities. These three [types of] action all have the characteristic of the nonconstructed. The body's characteristic of the nonconstructed is the same as speech's characteristic of the nonconstructed. Speech's characteristic of the nonconstructed is the same as the mind's characteristic of the nonconstructed. The characteristic of the nonconstructed of these three [types of] action is the same as the characteristic of the nonconstructed of all *dharma*s. To be able to be in accord with this wisdom of the nonconstructed is to enter the Dharma gate of nonduality."

25. Field of Blessings Bodhisattva said, "Meritorious action, transgressive action, and immobility constitute dualities. The real nature of these three [types of] action is emptiness. Emptiness is without meritorious action, transgressive action, and immobility. Not to generate these three [types of] action is to enter the Dharma gate of nonduality."

26. Flower Ornament Bodhisattva said, "The generation of dualities from the self constitutes a duality. To see the real characteristic of the self is to not generate dualistic *dharma*s. If one does not abide in dualistic *dharma*s, then there is no consciousness. To be without consciousness is to enter the Dharma gate of nonduality."

27. Store of Virtue Bodhisattva said, "The characteristics of the attainable (i.e., the perceptible) constitute dualities. If there is unattainability, then there is no grasping and forsaking. If there is no grasping and no forsaking, this is to enter the Dharma gate of nonduality."

551c

28. Superior Moon Bodhisattva said, "Darkness and illumination constitute a duality. If there is no darkness and no illumination,

then there is no duality. Why? If one enters into the concentration of extinction, there is no darkness and no illumination. The characteristics of all the *dharma*s are also like this. To enter this with universal sameness is to enter the Dharma gate of nonduality."

29. Jewel Seal Hand Bodhisattva said, "To delight in nirvana and not to delight in the world constitute a duality. If one does not delight in nirvana and does not have aversion for the world, then there is no duality. Why? If there is bondage, then there is emancipation. If there is fundamentally no bondage, who would seek emancipation? Without bondage or emancipation, then there is no delighting or aversion. This is to enter the Dharma gate of nonduality."

30. Crown of Pearls King Bodhisattva said, "The correct path and the heterodox paths constitute a duality. Those who abide in the correct path do not discriminate between the heterodox and the correct. To transcend this duality is to enter the Dharma gate of nonduality."

31. Delights in the Real Bodhisattva said, "The real and the unreal constitute a duality. To really see is not to see reality, and how much more so the not-real? Why? That which the physical eye cannot see can be seen by the wisdom eye, but this wisdom eye is without seeing and without not-seeing. This is to enter the Dharma gate of nonduality."

32. After the various bodhisattvas had thus each made their explanations, [Vimalakīrti] asked Mañjuśrī, "How does the bodhisattva enter the Dharma gate of nonduality?"

Mañjuśrī said, "As I understand it, it is to be without words and without explanation with regard to all the *dharma*s—without manifestation, without consciousness, and transcending all questions and answers. This is to enter the Dharma gate of nonduality."

33. Mañjuśrī then asked Vimalakīrti, "We have each made our own explanations. Sir, you should explain how the bodhisattva enters the Dharma gate of nonduality."

At this point Vimalakīrti was silent, saying nothing.

Mañjuśrī exclaimed, "Excellent, excellent! Not to even have words or speech is the true entrance into the Dharma gate of nonduality."

When this "Discourse on Entering the Dharma Gate of Nonduality" was explained, five thousand bodhisattvas within the congregation all entered the Dharma gate of nonduality and attained forbearance of the nonarising of *dharmas*.

End of Fascicle Two

Chapter X

The Buddha Accumulation
of Fragrances

1. At this point Śāriputra thought to himself, "It is almost noon. What will all these bodhisattvas eat?"

Then Vimalakīrti, knowing his thoughts, said, "The Buddha has explained the eight emancipations. You, sir, have accepted them as your practice. How can you mix up the desire for food and [that of] listening to the Dharma? If you wish to eat, then just wait a moment. I will provide you with an unprecedented meal."

2. Then Vimalakīrti entered into *samādhi* and, using his powers of numinous penetration, manifested to the great congregations that in the upper direction, past Buddha lands as numerous as the sands of forty-two Ganges Rivers, there was a country called Host of Fragrances, with a Buddha named Accumulation of Fragrances, who currently exists in that world. In comparison with the world-systems of the other Buddhas thoughout the ten directions, the fragrances [experienced by] the humans and gods of that country are supreme. In that land, the names *"śrāvaka"* and *"pratyekabuddha"* do not exist—there is only the great congregation of pure bodhisattvas, for whom the Buddha explains the Dharma. In that world all the buildings are made of fragrance. In doing walking meditation on that fragrant earth, the gardens are all fragrant. The fragrance of the food there circulates throughout the immeasurable worlds in the ten directions.

At the time, that Buddha and the bodhisattvas [in that country] were just sitting together to eat. The gods in attendance [in Vimalakīrti's assembly] all exclaimed at the ornament of fragrance, and they all generated the intention to achieve *anuttarā samyaksaṃbodhi,* making offerings to that Buddha and the bodhisattvas.

Everyone in the great congregations [in Vimalakīrti's room] saw this.

3. At that time, Vimalakīrti asked the congregation of bodhisattvas, "Sirs, who is able to go get food from that Buddha?"

Through the influence of Mañjuśrī's awesome numinous power, they all remained silent.

Vimalakīrti said, "Sir, are you not ashamed for this great congregation?"

Mañjuśrī said, "As the Buddha has said, one should not belittle those of no learning."

4. At this Vimalakīrti, without rising from his seat, created by transformation a bodhisattva whose [thirty-two primary] characteristics and [eighty subsidiary] marks were radiantly bright, whose glorious presence was particularly excellent, surpassing all in the assembly. [Vimalakīrti] announced to him, "Go to the world in the upper direction where, separated from here by Buddha lands as numerous as the sands of forty-two Ganges Rivers, there is a country named Host of Fragrances. The Buddha [of that country], named Accumulation of Fragrances, is just sitting down to eat with the bodhisattvas. Go there, and say as I tell you: 'Vimalakīrti bows his head to the feet of the World-honored One, and with great respect he inquires immeasurable times as to whether you might have some slight illness, some slight vexation, and whether your energies are at peace. He wishes to obtain the leftovers of the World-honored One's meal, which would be given to accomplish the Buddha's work in the Sahā world.

"'It will cause those who delight in inferior *dharma*s to disseminate the great path, and it will also cause the Tathāgata's (i.e., the Buddha Accumulation of Fragrances) reputation to be universally known.'"

552b

5. Then the conjured bodhisattva ascended to the upper direction in front of the assembly. The entire congregation saw him arrive at that Host of Fragrances world and worship at that Buddha's feet. They also heard him say,

"Vimalakīrti bows his head to the feet of the World-honored One, and with great respect he inquires immeasurable times as to whether you might have some slight illness, some slight vexation, and whether your energies are at peace. He wishes to obtain the leftovers of the World-honored One's meal, which would be given to accomplish the Buddha's work in the Sahā world.

"It will cause those who delight in inferior *dharma*s to disseminate the great path, and it will also cause the Tathāgata's reputation to be universally known."

6. When the great beings there saw the conjured bodhisattva, they exclaimed that it was unprecedented. "Where has this superior person come from? Where is the Sahā world? What does he mean, 'those who delight in inferior *dharma*s'?"

So did they question the Buddha [Accumulation of Fragrances], and that Buddha said, "In the lower direction, separated from here by Buddha lands as numerous as the sands of forty-two Ganges Rivers, is a world named Sahā. The Buddha there is named Śākya-muni, who exists at present in an evil age of five corruptions. He extensively disseminates the teaching of the path in order to enlighten those who delight in inferior *dharma*s. One of his bodhisattvas is named Vimalakīrti, who resides in the inconceivable emancipation and explains the Dharma for the bodhisattvas [of the Sahā world]. Therefore, he has sent this conjured [bodhisattva] here to praise my name and extol this land, so that those bodhisattvas will increase their merit."

7. The bodhisattvas there said, "How was he able to create this conjured [bodhisattva]? How great are his powers of merit, fearlessness, and the bases of numinous [power]?"

That Buddha said, "[Vimalakīrti's powers are] extremely great. He sends transformations to all the ten directions, where they carry out the Buddha's work and benefit sentient beings."

8. Then Accumulation of Fragrances Tathāgata gave his bowl with its host of fragrances and filled with fragrant food to the conjured bodhisattva.

The nine million bodhisattvas there then all spoke in unison, "We wish to proceed to the Sahā world to make offerings to Śākyamuni Buddha. We also wish to see Vimalakīrti and the other bodhisattva congregations."

The Buddha said, "You may go.

"However, withdraw the fragrance of your bodies, so as not to cause the sentient beings there to generate thoughts of deluded attachment. Also, you should forsake your original forms, so as not to cause those seeking to become bodhisattvas in that country to be ashamed of themselves. In addition, you must not harbor feelings of belittlement or thoughts of the hindrances [present in that world]. Why? The countries of the ten directions are all like space (i.e., devoid of fixed reality). Furthermore, [you should realize] that the Buddhas do not completely manifest their pure lands solely in order to convert those who delight in inferior *dharma*s."

9. Then, by means of the Buddha's awesome numinous [penetrations] and Vimalakīrti's power, the conjured bodhisattva took the bowl and food and, accompanied by those nine million bodhisattvas, suddenly disappeared from that world. In an instant, they arrived at Vimalakīrti's house.

552c   10. Vimalakīrti then created by transformation nine million lion seats, excellently ornamented as before, and the bodhisattvas all sat upon them.

The conjured bodhisattva gave the bowl full of fragrant food to Vimalakīrti.

The fragrance of the food wafted through Vaiśālī and the [whole] trimegachiliocosm.

When the brahmans and retired scholars of Vaiśālī smelled this fragrance, their bodies and minds were joyful, and they exclaimed at the unprecedented [event]. At this, Moon Canopy, the leader of the elders, followed by eighty-four thousand people, came and entered Vimalakīrti's house.

Seeing that the room contained so many lion seats, which were so tall and broad, with excellent ornamentation, in great joy they all worshiped the congregation of bodhisattvas and great disciples, then stood to one side. The earth spirits, sky spirits, and gods of the desire and form realms, smelling this fragrance, also entered Vimalakīrti's house.

11. Then Vimalakīrti said to Śāriputra and the other great *śrāvaka*s, "Sirs, you may eat the Tathāgata's food of the flavor of sweet dew, which is perfumed with the limitless intention of great compassion, and which will not be diminished by its consumption."

12. Another *śrāvaka* wondered, "There is not much of this food, yet everyone in the great assembly is supposed to eat!"

The conjured bodhisattva said, "Do not measure the limitless blessings and sagacity of the Tathāgata with the small merit and small wisdom of a *śrāvaka*! Even were the four seas to dry up, this food would not be exhausted. Even if everyone ate as much as [Mount] Sumeru for an entire *kalpa,* we would never be able to exhaust it. Why? That which is left over from the meal of someone who fully possesses the merits of morality, meditation, wisdom, sagacity, emancipation, and the vision and hearing of emancipation can never be exhausted."

13. At this, the bowl of food satisfied all within the assembly, yet was unchanged and undepleted. The bodhisattvas, *śrāvaka*s, gods, and humans who ate this food became physically peaceful and happy, as if they were all bodhisattvas who take pleasure in ornamenting their [Buddha] countries. Also, their pores all exuded wondrous fragrances, just like the fragrances of the trees of the Host of Fragrances country.

14. Vimalakīrti then asked the bodhisattvas from the Host of Fragrances [world], "How does Accumulation of Fragrances Tathāgata explain the Dharma?"

Those bodhisattvas said, "In our land the Tathāgata explains [the Dharma] without words. He simply uses the host of fragrances to make the gods and humans enter into the practice of the Vinaya. The bodhisattvas each sit beneath fragrant trees, smelling such wondrous fragrances, from which they attain the '*samādhi* of the repository of all virtues.' Those who attain this *samādhi* all become replete in the merits of the bodhisattva."

15. Those bodhisattvas asked Vimalakīrti, "Now, how does the World-honored One Śākyamuni explain the Dharma here?"

Vimalakīrti said, "The sentient beings of this land are obdurate and difficult to convert, and so the Buddha disciplines them by means of stern language.

"He says, 'These are the hells, these are the animals, and these are the hungry ghosts. These are the places of difficulty, and these are the places where the foolish are born.

553a "'These are licentious practices of the body, and these are the retributions for licentious practices of the body. These are licentious practices of the mouth, and these are the retributions for licentious practices of the mouth. These are licentious practices of the mind, and these are the retributions for licentious practices of the mind.

"'This is to kill sentient beings, and this is the retribution for killing sentient beings. This is to take what is not given, and this is the retribution for taking what is not given. This is licentiousness, and this is the retribution for licentiousness. This is false speech, and this is the retribution for false speech. This is slander, and this is the retribution for slander. This is defamation, and this is the retribution for defamation. This is meaningless speech, and this is the retribution for meaningless speech.

"'These are desire and jealousy, and this is the retribution for desire and jealousy. These are anger and vexation, and this is the retribution for anger and vexation. These are heterodox views, and this is the retribution for heterodox views. This is parsimony, and this is the retribution for parsimony. This is immorality (lit., "breaking the precepts"), and this is the retribution for immorality. This is anger, and this is the retribution for anger. This is laziness, and this is the retribution for laziness. This is perturbation, and this is the retribution for perturbation. This is stupidity, and this is the retribution for stupidity.

"'This is to be bound by the precepts, this is to maintain the precepts, and this is to transgress the precepts. This is what you should do, and this is what you should not do. These are hindrances, and these are not hindrances. These are transgressions, and these are not transgressions (lit., "transcend transgression"). This is pure, and this is defiled. This is to have flaws, and this is to be flawless. This is the wrong path, and this is the correct path. This is the conditioned, and this is the unconditioned. This is worldly, and this is nirvana.'

"Since the minds of people so difficult to convert are like monkeys, one must use several types of Dharma to control their minds, so that they can be disciplined. It is like elephants and horses who are stubborn and uncontrollable, who can only be disciplined by making them suffer to the bone. Because the sentient beings [of this world] are obdurate like this, [Śākyamuni] uses all sorts of painfully strict language to get [sentient beings] to enter into the Vinaya."

16. When those bodhisattvas heard this explanation, they all said, "How unprecedented! Thus the World-honored One Śākyamuni Buddha conceals his immeasurable autonomous powers and uses that which is enjoyed by the poverty-stricken to save sentient beings. The bodhisattvas here are also able to labor and be humble, and it is with immeasurable great compassion that they have been born in this Buddha land."

Vimalakīrti said, "The bodhisattvas of this land are resolute in their compassion for the sentient beings here. Truly, it is as you have said. Thus in a single lifetime they benefit more sentient beings than you do in that country (i.e., the Host of Fragrances world) in a hundred thousand *kalpa*s of practice. Why?

17. "This Sahā world has ten excellent *dharma*s (i.e., features) that are lacking in the other pure lands. What are these ten?

    i) "The poor are attracted by charity,

    ii) "the transgressors are attracted by pure precepts,

    iii) "the angry are attracted by forbearance,

    iv) "the lazy are attracted by exertion,

    v) "the perturbed are attracted by meditation,

    vi) "the foolish are attracted by wisdom,

vii) "those who experience the eight difficulties are saved by explanation of how to eliminate difficulties,

viii) "those who take pleasure in the Hinayana are saved by the teaching of the Mahayana,

ix) "those without merit may be saved by the various good roots, and

x) "[the liberation of] sentient beings is constantly being accomplished by means of the four attractions.

"These are the ten."

18. Those bodhisattvas said, "How many *dharma*s do bodhisattvas have to accomplish in their flawless practice in this world to be born in a pure land?"

553b   Vimalakīrti said, "Bodhisattvas accomplish eight *dharma*s in their flawless practice in this world so as to be born in a pure land. What are the eight?

i) "They benefit sentient beings without seeking recompense,

ii) "they experience various sufferings in place of all sentient beings,

iii) "they donate all the merit from their actions to others,

iv) "in humility and non-interference they are even-minded toward all sentient beings,

v) "they view [other] bodhisattvas as if they were Buddhas,

vi) "they hear and do not doubt sutras they have not heard before,

vii) "they do not become refractory toward *śrāvaka*s, and

viii) "they are not jealous of the offerings [received by] others and do not become haughty over benefit to themselves.

"In these [eight *dharma*s] they discipline their minds, always reflecting on their own errors and not proclaiming the shortcomings of others, yet always singlemindedly seeking the various merits. These are the eight *dharma*s."

When Vimalakīrti and Mañjuśrī explained this Dharma to the great congregation, a hundred thousand gods and humans all generated the intention to achieve *anuttarā samyaksaṃbodhi,* and ten thousand bodhisattvas attained the forbearance of the nonarising of *dharma*s.

Chapter XI

Practices of the Bodhisattva

1. Meanwhile, the Buddha had been explaining the Dharma in the garden of Āmrapālī. The land there suddenly expanded and became ornamented, and the entire assembly became gold in color.

Ānanda asked the Buddha, "World-honored One, due to what causes and conditions are there these propitious responses? This place has suddenly expanded and became ornamented, and the entire assembly has become gold in color!"

The Buddha told Ānanda, "This is because Vimalakīrti and Mañjuśrī, together with the great congregations that surround and revere them, will decide they want to come here. It is in anticipation of this that these propitious responses have occurred."

2. Just then Vimalakīrti said to Mañjuśrī, "We should go together to see the Buddha, to revere him and make offerings along with the bodhisattvas."

Mañjuśrī said, "Excellent! Let us go. This is just the right time."

Vimalakīrti, using his numinous power, lifted the great congregations together with the lion seats in his right hand and proceeded to where the Buddha was. When he arrived there he placed them on the ground. He bowed his head to the Buddha's feet, then circumambulated him seven times. Holding his palms together singlemindedly, he then stood to one side.

The bodhisattvas all left their seats and bowed their heads to the Buddha's feet, then circumambulated him seven times, and stood to one side. The great disciples, Śakras, Brahmās, four heavenly kings, and so on, also all left their seats to bow their heads to the Buddha's feet, and then stood to one side.

Then the World-honored One, according to custom, requested

that the bodhisattvas all sit once again. They all followed these instructions, and the congregation sat and became settled.

3. The Buddha said to Śāriputra, "Have you seen what this bodhisattva, this great being, has done with his autonomous numinous power?"

[Śāriputra said,] "Yes, I have seen."

[The Buddha said,] "What do you think about it?"

[Śāriputra said,] "World-honored One, I look upon what has been done as inconceivable. It is something that my mind cannot figure out and which my powers cannot even estimate."

4. Then Ānanda addressed the Buddha, "World-honored One, the fragrance I smell now is one I have never experienced before. What fragrance is it?"

The Buddha told Ānanda, "This is the fragrance from the pores of those bodhisattvas."

Then Śāriputra said to Ānanda, "Our pores are also emitting this fragrance."

Ānanda said, "Where does it come from?"

[Śāriputra] said, "This elder, Vimalakīrti, brought the leftover meal from the Buddha of the Host of Fragrances country to his house [for us to] eat, and so all our pores are fragrant like this."

5. Ānanda asked Vimalakīrti, "How long will this fragrance last?"

Vimalakīrti said, "Until the food is digested."

[Ānanda] said, "When will the food be digested?"

[Vimalakīrti] said, "The energy of this food will be digested after seven days.

6. "Also, Ānanda:

i) "If a *śrāvaka* who has not yet entered the primary status [of Hinayana enlightenment] eats this food, it will only be digested after he enters the primary status.

ii) "If someone who has already entered the primary status eats this food, it will only be digested after his mind is emancipated.

iii) "If someone who has not generated the intention [to follow the] Mahayana eats this food, it will only be digested after he has generated that intention.

176

iv) "If someone who has already generated the [Mahayana] intention eats this food, it will only be digested after he has attained forbearance of the birthlessness of *dharmas*.

v) "If someone who has already attained forbearance of the nonarising of *dharmas* eats this food, it will only be digested after he has reached his penultimate rebirth.

vi) "It is as if there were a medicine called 'superior flavor' that is digested only after all the poisons in the body of the person who takes it have been eliminated.

7. "Like this, this food eliminates all the poisons of the afflictions and then is digested."

Ānanda addressed the Buddha, "This is unprecedented! World-honored One, can fragrant food perform the Buddha's work like this?"

The Buddha said, "Just so, just so, Ānanda.

8. "There are Buddha lands where the illumination of the Buddha performs the Buddha's work, or where the bodhisattvas perform the Buddha's work, or where conjured persons created by the Buddha perform the Buddha's work, or where the *bodhi* tree performs the Buddha's work, or where the Buddha's clothing and bedding perform the Buddha's work, or where food performs the Buddha's work, or where groves and pavilions perform the Buddha's work, or where the thirty-two characteristics and eighty subsidiary marks perform the Buddha's work, or where the Buddha's body performs the Buddha's work, or where space performs the Buddha's work. Sentient beings respond to these conditions and are able to enter into the practice of the Vinaya.

9. "There are [other Buddha lands] where dreams, phantasms, shadows, echos, images in mirrors, the moon [reflected in] water, mirages during times of heat, and other metaphors perform the Buddha's work; or where sounds, words, and letters perform the Buddha's work; or where a pure Buddha land is serene and silent, where the wordless, the explanationless, the manifestationless, the consciousnessless, the unconstructed, and the unconditioned perform the Buddha's work.

10. "Thus, Ānanda, given the Buddhas' deployment of the deportments and their various actions, there is nothing that is not the Buddha's work.

"Ānanda, there may occur these eighty-four thousand gate-

ways of affliction of the four Māras, which trouble sentient beings.

11. "The Buddhas use these *dharmas* to perform the Buddha's work—this is called 'to enter into the Dharma gates of all the Buddhas.'

"When bodhisattvas enter these gates, even if they see all the pure and excellent Buddha lands they do not become happy, do not desire them, and do not become elated; even if they see all the impure Buddha lands, they do not become sad, do not become hindered, and do not become melancholy. They merely generate pure minds with regard to the Buddhas, being joyful and respectful toward the unprecedented [teachings they encounter].

"The merits of the Buddhas, the Tathāgatas, are universally same, and it is in order to convert sentient beings that they manifest different Buddha lands.

12. "Ānanda, when you observe the Buddhas' countries, the lands are numerous but space is not (i.e., there is only one "space"). Likewise, when you observe the form bodies of the Buddhas, they are numerous but their unhindered wisdom is not.

13. "Ānanda, regarding the Buddhas' form bodies; their awesome characteristics and qualities; their morality, meditation, wisdom, emancipation, knowledge and vision of emancipation; their powers, fearlessnesses, [and other] exclusive attributes [of the Buddhas]; their great sympathy, great compassion, and the practices of the deportments; their lifespan, explanation of the Dharma, and teaching; and their purification of Buddha countries where they accomplish [the emancipation of] sentient beings—

"all [the Buddhas] are identically replete in all these Buddha-Dharmas. Therefore, they are called *samyaksaṃbuddha,* they are called *tathāgata,* they are called *buddha.*

"Ānanda, if I were to explain the meanings of these three [Sanskrit] phrases extensively, you would not be able to experience them completely even if you had the lifespan of a *kalpa*! Even if all the sentient beings in the trimegachiliocosm were, like Ānanda, paramount in erudition, and retained them mindfully with *dhāraṇī*, and even if they had lifespans of a *kalpa,* they would not be able to experience them completely! Thus it is, Ānanda, that the *anuttarā samyaksaṃbodhi* of the Buddhas is limitless, and their wisdom and eloquence is inconceivable!"

14. Ānanda addressed the Buddha, "From now on I will not be able to consider myself erudite."

The Buddha told Ānanda, "Do not become discouraged. Why? I have explained that you are the most erudite among the *śrāvaka*s. I did not say [among the] bodhisattvas. But stop, Ānanda! The wise should not [attempt to] evaluate the bodhisattvas. How could the total depth of the ocean be calculated? All the merits of the bodhisattvas' meditation, wisdom, *dhāraṇī,* and eloquence are immeasurable.

"Ānanda, you [*śrāvaka*s] have forsaken the practices of the bodhisattva. The power of numinous penetration that Vimalakīrti has manifested on this one occasion would be impossible for *śrāvaka*s or *pratyekabuddha*s to do by their powers of transformation even in a hundred thousand *kalpa*s."

15. At that time the bodhisattvas who had come from the Host of Fragrances world held their palms together and addressed the Buddha, "World-honored One, when we first saw this land we generated the concept of its inferiority. Now we are ashamed of ourselves and have abandoned this attitude. Why? The skillful means 554b of the Buddhas are inconceivable. In order to save sentient beings, they manifest different Buddha countries in accordance with the responses of [sentient beings].

"Please, O World-honored One, bestow upon us a bit of your Dharma as we return to the other world, so that we might remember you."

16. The Buddha told the bodhisattvas, "You should learn the teaching of the emancipation of the exhaustible and inexhaustible. What is the exhaustible?

"It is the conditioned *dharma*s. What is the inexhaustible? It is the unconditioned *dharma*s. If you are bodhisattvas, you should neither exhaust the conditioned nor abide in the unconditioned.

17. "What is it not to exhaust the conditioned? It is neither to transcend great sympathy nor to forsake great compassion, to profoundly generate the aspiration to achieve omniscience and never forget it even momentarily. It is to teach sentient beings without ever becoming tired, to be constantly mindful of following the teaching of the four attractions. It is to defend the correct Dharma without fear for one's own life, to plant good roots without becoming fatigued. It is for one's intent to always be on peaceful abiding and one's skillful means rededicated [to *anuttarā samyaksaṃbodhi*]. It is to seek the Dharma without tiring and explain the Dharma without parsimony, and to energetically make offerings to the Buddhas.

"By doing so one will enter samsara without fear, be without sadness or joy regarding the various honors and disgraces, not belittle the unlearned and revere the learned as if they are Buddhas, cause those who have fallen into the afflictions to generate correct mindfulness, distantly transcend pleasure and not consider it valuable, not be attached to one's own pleasure yet celebrate the pleasure of others, have the concept that being in the *dhyāna*s is like being in the hells, and have the concept that being in samsara is like being in a garden or pavilion.

"One will have the concept that seeing one coming to make a request is like [seeing] an excellent teacher, have the concept that to forsake one's various possessions is to be replete in omniscience, have the concept that to see transgressors is to generate salvific protection, have the concept of the *pāramitā*s (perfections) being one's parents, and have the concept of the [thirty-seven] factors of enlightenment being one's subordinates. One's generation of practices and [planting of] good roots will be limitless. One will create one's own Buddha land with the various ornamentations of the pure countries [of different Buddhas].

"Practicing limitless charity, one will become replete in the [thirty-two primary] characteristics and [eighty subsidiary] marks.

Eliminating all evil, one will purify one's body, speech, and mind. Being born and dying for countless *kalpa*s, one will remain courageous [throughout]. Hearing of the immeasurable merits and intention of the Buddhas, one will never become tired. With the sword of wisdom one will destroy the 'bandits' of the afflictions, and one will emerge from the *skandha*s, realms (*dhātu*s), and entrances (*āyatana*s).

"One will bear the burden of sentient beings and always make them become emancipated. With great exertion one will subjugate the armies of Māra. One will always seek the practice of wisdom of the real characteristic of no-mindfulness. One will know satisfaction through minimal desire regarding the worldly *dharma*s. One will seek the supramundane *dharma*s without tiring. Yet one will be able to accord with the profane, without either forsaking the worldly *dharma*s or breaking the deportments. One will generate the sagacity of numinous penetration and entice sentient beings [to salvation]. One will not forget what one has heard through the *dhāraṇī* of memory. One will discriminate well [between] those of the various capacities and eliminate the doubts of sentient beings. One will expound upon the Dharma without hindrance, taking pleasure in one's eloquence. One will be pure in carrying out the ten types of good and experience the blessing of gods and humans. One will cultivate the four unlimiteds and open up the path to the Brahmā heavens. One will exhort and request [others to] explain the Dharma and be accordingly joyous in praising its excellence.

"Attaining the Buddha's voice, one will be good in [acts of] body, 554c speech, and mind. Attaining the deportments of the Buddha, one will profoundly cultivate the good qualities, with one's practice becoming increasingly excellent. With the Mahayana teaching, one will become a bodhisattva monk. Without mental laxity, one will not fail in the host of goods. Practicing a Dharma such as this, one is called 'a bodhisattva who does not exhaust the conditioned.'

18. "What is a bodhisattva who does not abide in the unconditioned?

"It is to cultivate [the emancipation of the] empty without taking the empty as one's realization. It is to cultivate [the emancipations of] signlessness and wishlessness without taking the signless and the wishless as one's realization. It is to cultivate nonactivation without taking nonactivation as one's realization. It is to contemplate impermanence without having aversion for the roots of goodness. It is to contemplate worldly suffering without considering samsara evil. It is to contemplate no-self while teaching people without tiring. It is to contemplate extinction without undergoing permanent extinction. It is to contemplate transcendence while cultivating the good with mind and body.

"It is to contemplate the absence of any refuge while going for refuge in the *dharma*s of goodness. It is to contemplate the birthless, yet to bear the burden for all [sentient beings] using the *dharma*s of birth. It is to contemplate the flawless, yet not eliminate the flaws. It is to contemplate the absence of any practice, yet to teach sentient beings using the *dharma*s of practice. It is to contemplate emptiness and nonexistence, yet not to forsake great compassion. It is to contemplate the position of the correct Dharma, yet not to follow the Hinayana.

"It is to contemplate the empty falsity of the *dharma*s, which are without solidity, without selfhood, without subject, and without characteristic. It is not to consider merit, meditation, and wisdom to be in vain when one's original vow has not been fulfilled. Practicing a Dharma such as this, one is called 'a bodhisattva who does not abide in the unconditioned.'

19. "Furthermore, in order to be complete in merit one should not abide in the unconditioned; and in order to be complete in wisdom one should not exhaust the conditioned.

"In order to [achieve] great sympathy and compassion, one should not abide in the unconditioned; in order to fulfill one's original vow, one should not exhaust the conditioned. In order to accumulate the medicines of the Dharma, one should not abide in the unconditioned; in order to bestow medicines according [to the needs of sentient beings], one should not exhaust the conditioned. In order to understand the illnesses of sentient beings, one should not abide in the unconditioned; in order to extinguish the illnesses of sentient beings, one should not exhaust the conditioned. O good sirs, a bodhisattva who cultivates this Dharma does not either exhaust the conditioned or abide in the unconditioned. This is called 'the teaching of the emancipation of the exhaustible and inexhaustible.' You should learn this."

20. When those bodhisattvas heard the explanation of this Dharma they were all extremely happy, and they scattered hosts of wondrous flowers of several colors and fragrances throughout the trimegachiliocosm, making offerings to the Buddha, this teaching, and the bodhisattvas [of this world]. They bowed their heads to the Buddha's feet and exclaimed at this unprecedented [teaching], saying, "Śākyamuni Buddha is able to perform the skillful means of this excellent practice in this [world]." Saying this, they suddenly disappeared, returning to that other country.

Chapter XII

Vision of Akṣobhya Buddha

1. At this point the World-honored One asked Vimalakīrti, "When you wish to see the Tathāgata, in what ways do you view the Tathāgata?"

Vimalakīrti said, "As if contemplating the real characteristic of my own body—so do I view the Buddha.

"When I view the Tathāgata, he does not come in the past, does not go in the future, and does not abide in the present.

"I neither view him as form, nor view him as the suchness of form, nor view him as the nature of form. I neither view him as feeling, conception, process, or consciousness; nor view him as the suchness of consciousness; nor view him as the nature of consciousness.

"He does not arise from the four great elements and is identical to space. He has no accumulation of the six sensory capacities, and his eyes, ears, nose, tongue, body, and mind have already passed beyond and are not within the triple world.

"Having transcended the three defilements, he is in accord with the three emancipations. Complete in the three illuminations, he is equivalent to ignorance.

"He is neither the single characteristic nor different characteristics. He is neither a self-characteristic nor an other-characteristic. He is neither without characteristics, nor does he grasp characteristics.

"He is not of this shore, nor of the other shore, nor of the current [of samsara] in between, yet he converts sentient beings. I view him in extinction, yet he is not permanently in extinction. He is neither this nor that, and he neither uses this nor uses that.

555a

185

"He cannot be understood with wisdom, nor can he be known by consciousness. He is without darkness (i.e., ignorance), without brightness (i.e., understanding), without name, and without characteristic. He is without strength, without weakness, and neither pure nor defiled. He does not occupy a region, nor does he transcend the regions.

"He is neither conditioned nor unconditioned. He is without manifesting and without explaining.

"He is neither charitable nor stingy, neither observant nor transgressive [of the precepts], neither forbearant nor angry, neither energetic nor lazy, neither composed nor perturbed, and neither wise nor foolish. He is neither sincere nor dissembling, neither coming nor going, neither exiting nor entering. All the paths of words are eliminated.

"He is neither a field of blessings nor not a field of blessings. He is neither one worthy of offerings (i.e., arhat) nor not one worthy of offerings.

"He neither grasps nor forsakes; he neither has characteristics nor is without characteristics.

"He is identical to the true limit and equivalent to the Dharma-nature.

"He is indescribable, incalculable; he transcends appellations and measures. He is neither great nor small.

"He is neither vision, nor hearing, nor perceiving, nor knowing; he transcends the host of fetters. He is equivalent to the various types of wisdom and identical to sentient beings. He is without discrimination with regard to the *dharmas*.

"He is entirely without failing, without impurity, without vexation, without intentionality (lit., "unconstructed"), without activation, without generation, and without extinction; without fear, without sorrow, without joy, without dislike, and without attachment; without past, without future, and without present. He cannot be discriminated or manifested using any verbal explanations at all.

"World-honored One, such is the body of the Tathāgata, and thus do I perform its contemplation. To use this contemplation is called the correct contemplation. If [one uses some] other contemplation, this is called the incorrect contemplation."

2. Śāriputra then asked Vimalakīrti, "Where did you die to become born here?"

Vimalakīrti said, "Are there death and birth in the *dharmas* as you apprehend (lit., "attain") them?"

Śāriputra said, "There are no death and birth [in the *dharmas*]."

[Vimalakīrti said,] "If the *dharmas* are without the characteristics of death and birth, why do you ask 'Where did you die to become born here?' What do you mean? It is as if a magician conjures up a man and a woman—do they die and become born?"

Śāriputra said, "They do not die and become born."

[Vimalakīrti said,] "But can you not have heard the Buddha explain that the *dharmas* are like conjured characteristics?" 555b

[Śāriputra said,] "So I have."

[Vimalakīrti said,] "If all the *dharmas* are like conjured characteristics, why do you ask 'Where did you die to become born here?' Śāriputra, death is the characteristic of the destruction of false *dharmas*, and birth is the characteristic of continuity of false *dharmas*. Although bodhisattvas die, they do not exhaust their roots of goodness, and although they are born they do not nurture the various evils."

3. Then the Buddha told Śāriputra, "There is a country called Wondrous Joy (Abhirati), where the Buddha is entitled Akṣobhya (Immovable). Vimalakīrti died in that country prior to being born here."

Śāriputra said, "This is unprecedented! World-honored One, this person is able to forsake a pure land and come take pleasure in this place of great anger and harm."

Vimalakīrti said to Śāriputra, "What do you think? When the sun's light appears, is it conjoined with darkness?"

[Śāriputra] answered, "No. When the sun's light appears, the darkness disappears."

Vimalakīrti said, "Why does the sun come to Jambudvīpa?"

[Śāriputra] answered, "To illuminate it and eliminate the darkness."

Vimalakīrti said, "Bodhisattvas are like this. Even though they are born in impure Buddha lands in order to convert sentient beings, they are not therefore conjoined with the darkness of stupidity. They merely extinguish the darkness of the afflictions of sentient beings."

4. At this time the great congregation eagerly wished to see the Wondrous Joy world, Akṣobhya Tathāgata, and his congregations of bodhisattvas and *śrāvaka*s.

Knowing what the entire assembly was thinking, [the Buddha] told Vimalakīrti, "Good man, on behalf of this assembly, manifest Wondrous Joy world, Akṣobhya Tathāgata, and his congregations of bodhisattvas and *śrāvaka*s. The congregations all wish to see them."

Vimalakīrti then thought to himself, "Without getting up from my seat I should lift the Wondrous Joy world, including its Iron Ring Mountains; streams, rivers, oceans, springs; [Mount] Sumeru and the other mountains; the sun, moon, and stars; the palaces of the gods, dragons, demonic spirits, and Brahmā gods; its congregations of bodhisattvas and *śrāvaka*s; the cities, towns, villages, men and women, adults and childen; and even Akṣobhya Tathāgata with the *bodhi* tree and its wondrous lotus flowers, which are able to perform the Buddha's work throughout the ten directions. There are three jeweled stairways from Jambudvīpa to the Tuṣita Heaven, and the gods descend these jeweled stairways. They all worship Akṣobhya Tathāgata and listen to his Dharma. The people of Jambudvīpa also climb those stairways, ascending to Tuṣita to see the gods there.

"The Wondrous Joy world is composed of such immeasurable merits, from the Akaniṣṭha Heaven above to the water limit (i.e., the disk of water) below. I will grasp it in my right hand, as a potter does a wheel, bringing it into this world like carrying a flower garland, to show all the congregations."

5. Thinking this thought, [Vimalakīrti] entered *samādhi* and manifested the power of numinous transformation. With his right hand he grasped the Wondrous Joy world and placed it in this land.

555c

6. Those congregations of bodhisattvas and *śrāvaka*s [in that Wondrous Joy world], as well as the other gods and humans who had attained numinous penetration, all said, "O World-honored One, who is taking us away? Please save us!"

Akṣobhya Buddha said, "This is not my doing. This is being done through the numinous power of Vimalakīrti."

The others, who had not attained numinous penetration, were unaware of where they were going.

Although the Wondrous Joy world entered this land, it did not expand or contract. At this the [Sahā] world was not constricted, but unchanged from before.

7. At this point Śākyamuni Buddha told the great congregations, "You may view the Wondrous Joy world, Akṣobhya Tathāgata, and the ornamentations of that country, and the pure practices of the bodhisattvas and purity of the disciples."

They all said, "Yes, we see them."

The Buddha said, "Bodhisattvas who wish to attain pure Buddha lands such as this should learn the path that has been practiced by Akṣobhya Tathāgata."

When this Wondrous Joy world was manifested, fourteen *nayutas* of people in the Sahā world generated the intention to achieve *anuttarā samyaksaṃbodhi,* all wishing to be born in the Wondrous Joy Buddha land. Śākyamuni Buddha predicted for them, saying, "You will be born in that country."

Then the benefits in response of having the Wondrous Joy world in this country were finished, and it returned to its original place, as seen by the entire congregation.

8. The Buddha told Śāriputra, "Did you see this Wondrous Joy world and Akṣobhya Buddha?"

[Śāriputra said,] "Yes, I saw them. World-honored One, I wish that every sentient being could attain a pure land like that of Akṣobhya Buddha and obtain the power of numinous penetration like Vimalakīrti.

"World-honored One, we have quickly attained good benefit, seeing these people and making offerings directly to them. Those sentient beings who hear this sutra, either now [while you are] present or after the Buddha's nirvana, will also attain good benefit. How much more so if, after hearing it, they devoutly understand, accept, recite, explain, and practice according to it!

9. "Those who get hold of this sutra will attain the [entire] storehouse (i.e., treasury) of the Dharma jewel.

"If one reads, recites, explains its meaning, or practices according to its explanation, one will be protected and remembered by the Buddhas. To make offerings to such a person—understand that this is to make offerings to the Buddha. To copy and maintain these fascicles of scripture—understand that the Tathāgata is present in that room. Those who hear this sutra and are able to become joyful accordingly will achieve omniscience. If one is able to devoutly understand this sutra, even just a single four-phrase verse (*gāthā*), and explain it to others—understand that such people will immediately receive a prediction of [their future achievement of] *anut-*
tarā samyaksaṃbodhi."

Chapter XIII

Dharma Offering

1. At this time Śakra Devānām Indra, who was in the great congregation, announced to the Buddha, "World-honored One, although I have listened to a hundred thousand sutras by yourself and Mañjuśrī, I had never heard this scripture of the definitive true characteristic of the inconceivable, autonomous, numinous penetration.

2. "According to my understanding of the meaning explained by you, if there are sentient beings who hear this sutra and who devoutly understand, accept and maintain, and read and recite it, they will definitely attain this Dharma, and will not doubt it. How much more so if they cultivate according to its explanation! Such people will immediately close off the host of evil destinations and open the gateways of good. They will always be protected and remembered by the Buddhas. They will subjugate the heterodox teachings and demolish the vengeful Māras. They will cultivate *bodhi* and reside peacefully in the place of enlightenment. They will walk in the very footsteps the Tathāgata has trod.

3. "World-honored One, if there are those who accept and maintain, read and recite, and cultivate [this sutra] as it has explained, I and my subordinates will make offerings and serve them.

"As to the villages, towns, mountain forests, and wildernesses where this sutra is found, I and my subordinates will go to those locations in order to listen to the Dharma. I will cause those who do not yet believe to believe, and those who already believe will be protected."

4. The Buddha said, "Excellent, excellent! Heavenly emperor, it is as you have spoken. I am happy for you!

"This sutra extensively explains the inconceivable *anuttarā samyaksaṃbodhi* of the Buddhas of the past, present, and future. Therefore, heavenly emperor, if good men and women accept and maintain, read and recite, and make offerings to this sutra, that is tantamount to making offerings to the Buddhas of the past, present, and future.

5. "Heavenly emperor, even if the entire trimegachiliocosm were filled with Tathāgatas as numerous as the sugar cane, bamboo, reeds, rice, hemp, and forests, and if a good man or woman were to revere, honor, praise, make offerings, and provide all their needs for a *kalpa* or even less than a *kalpa,* until after the nirvana of those Tathāgatas;

"After [the nirvana of those Tathāgatas], if he or she erected a stupa of the seven treasures above the relics of every one of those Tathāgatas' bodies, as long and wide as a single fourfold world and as tall as the Brahmā heaven, [with each stupa constituting] a field ornamented with all [manner of] flowers, incense, garlands, banners, and musicians, paramount in most subtle wonder; and

"If [that good man or woman] made offerings to [these stupas] for a *kalpa* or less than a *kalpa*—

"What do you think, heavenly emperor? Would the blessings planted by that person be great or not?"

Śakra Devānām Indra said, "They would be great, World-honored One! One could not fully explain their merit, even in a hundred thousand *koṭi*s of *kalpa*s."

6. The Buddha told the heavenly emperor, "You should understand, the good man or woman who hears this scripture of the inconceivable emancipation and who devoutly understands, accepts, recites, and practices it will have blessings even greater than the former person.

"Why? The enlightenment of all the Buddhas is born from this.
556b The characteristic of *bodhi* is immeasurable, and based on this the blessings are immeasurable."

7. The Buddha told the heavenly emperor, "At a time immeasurable *asaṃkhyeya*s of *kalpa*s in the past, there was a Buddha

named Medicine King (Bhaiṣajyarāja), a Tathāgata, Arhat, Fully Enlightened One, One Endowed with Wisdom and Conduct, Well-gone One, Knower of the World, Supreme Master of Discipline, Teacher of Gods and Humans, Buddha, and World-honored One. His world was called Great Ornamentation. His *kalpa* was called Ornamentation.

"That Buddha's lifespan was twenty small *kalpa*s.

"He had a *śrāvaka* sangha of thirty-six *koṭi*s of *nayuta*s [of members], and a bodhisattva sangha of twelve *koṭi*s.

"Heavenly emperor, at the time there was a wheel-turning sage king named Jeweled Canopy, who was endowed with the seven treasures [of the *cakravartin*] and ruled the fourfold world. The king had one thousand sons, who were handsome, courageous, and able to subjugate their enemies.

8. "At the time Jeweled Canopy and his subordinates made offerings to Medicine King Tathāgata, providing all that he needed for a full five *kalpa*s. After five *kalpa*s he told his thousand sons, 'You should also make offerings to the Buddha with a profound mind, like me.' Then the thousand sons, accepting their father's order, made offerings to Medicine King Tathāgata, and they provided for his needs for another full five *kalpa*s.

9. "One of those sons, named Moon Canopy, sat alone, thinking 'Might there be some offering that would exceed even this?'

"Through the Buddha's numinous power, a god's voice was heard from space, 'Good man, the offering of the Dharma surpasses all other offerings.'

"[Moon Canopy] then asked, 'What is an offering of the Dharma?'

"The god said, 'You may go ask Medicine King Tathāgata. He will give you an extensive explanation of offerings of the Dharma.' Prince Moon Canopy immediately proceeded to Medicine King Tathāgata and bowed to his feet, then stood to one side and addressed the Buddha, 'World-honored One, of all the offerings, offerings of the Dharma are superior. What are offerings of the Dharma?'

10. The Buddha [Medicine King] said, "Good man, offerings of the Dharma are those made to the profound sutras explained by the Buddhas.

"In all the worlds, these are difficult to believe in, difficult to accept. They are subtle and difficult to see, pure and without defilement. They cannot be attained with only discriminative thinking.

"They are contained in the storehouse of the Dharma of the bodhisattvas. They are sealed by the seal of *dhāraṇī*. They take one to [the stage of] nonretrogression and to the accomplishment of the six perfections.

"They discriminate the meanings well, and they accord with the *dharma* of *bodhi*. They are supreme among the host of sutras and induct one into great sympathy and compassion. They transcend the affairs of the hosts of Māras and the various heterodox views. They accord with the *dharma* of causes and conditions.

11. "They are without self, without person, without sentient being, without lifespan. They [teach the three emancipations of] emptiness, signlessness, wishlessness and nonactivation.

"They are able to make sentient beings take their seat in the place of enlightenment and turn the wheel of the Dharma.

"They are praised by all the gods, dragons, [demonic] spirits (*yakṣas*), *gandharvas*, and so on.

"They are able to make sentient beings enter the store[house] of the Buddha-Dharma.

"They accommodate all the [types of] wisdom of the worthies and sages. They explain the path practiced by the host of bodhisattvas. They rely on the meanings of the true characteristic of the *dharmas*. They illuminate the *dharmas* of impermanence, 556c suffering, emptiness, no-self, and extinction.

"They are able to save all sentient beings who commit infractions. They can render afraid the Māras, heretics, and those attached to desire.

"They are praised by all the Buddhas, worthies, and sages. They reject the suffering of samsara and reveal the joy of nirvana.

They are explained by all the Buddhas of the ten directions and three periods of time.

"One who hears such sutras, and devoutly understands, accepts and maintains, and reads and recites them, will with the power of skillful means explain them clearly and with discriminative understanding for sentient beings. This is because that person will be maintaining and protecting the Dharma. This is called the 'offering of the Dharma.'

12. "Furthermore, when one practices as is explained in the Dharma, one will be in accord with the twelve [factors of] causes and conditions, transcend the heterodox views, and attain forbearance of the birthlessness of *dharma*s. There is definitively no self and no sentient beings, and within the retributive results of the causes and conditions there [will be in such persons] no disagreement, no contention, and the transcendence of all the qualities of self.

"They will rely on meanings, not on words. They will rely on wisdom, not on knowledge. They will rely on sutras of comprehensive meaning and not rely on sutras of incomplete meaning. They will rely on the Dharma and not rely on a person. They will be in accord with the characteristics of the Dharma, without anywhere that is entered, without any refuge. Ignorance will be thoroughly extinguished, and hence the processes will be thoroughly extinguished. Thus birth will be thoroughly extinguished, and hence old age and death will be thoroughly extinguished.

"If one performs such a contemplation, the twelve [factors of] causes and conditions will be without the characteristic of being exhausted. One will not generate views again. This is called the 'offering of the supreme Dharma.'"

13. The Buddha told the heavenly emperor, "When Prince Moon Canopy heard this Dharma from Medicine King Buddha, he attained the forbearance of compliance. Taking off his jeweled robe and bodily ornaments, he offered them to the Buddha, saying 'World-honored One, after your nirvana I will practice the offering of the Dharma and defend the correct Dharma. Please use your

numinous charisma compassionately, so that I will be able to subjugate the vengeful Māras and cultivate the practices of the bodhisattva.'"

Knowing the profound thoughts in [the prince's] mind, [Medicine King] Buddha made the prediction, "At the very end, you will defend the Dharma city."

14. [The Buddha told the] heavenly emperor, "Prince Moon Canopy then saw the purity of the Dharma. Hearing the Buddha bestow a prediction [of future Buddhahood] on him, he developed faith and left home. After cultivating the good Dharma with exertion for not very long, he attained the five numinous penetrations and became a bodhisattva. He attained *dhāraṇī* and unending eloquence. After the nirvana of that Buddha, using the power of the numinous penetrations, *dhāraṇī,* and eloquence that he had attained, he disseminated the wheel of the Dharma that Medicine King Buddha had turned for a full ten short *kalpas*. Through his diligent practice and exertion in defending the Dharma, in that lifetime Moon Canopy *bhikṣu* converted a million *koṭi*s of people, who became irreversible in their [quest for] *anuttarā samyaksaṃbodhi*. Fourteen *nayuta*s of people generated the profound inspiration to become *śrāvaka*s and *pratyekabuddha*s. Immeasurable sentient beings gained birth in the heavens.

"Heavenly emperor, was not the Prince Jeweled Canopy of that time an unusual person! As of now he has attained Buddhahood and is entitled Jewel Mirage Tathāgata. Those thousand princes became the thousand Buddhas of the *bhadrakalpa*. The first achieved Buddhahood as Krakucchandra, and the last will be the Tathāgata named Ruci. Moon Canopy *bhikṣu* was I myself.

15. "Thus, heavenly emperor, you should understand this essential point: the offering of the Dharma excels all other offerings. It is supreme, incomparable. Therefore, heavenly emperor, you should use the offering of the Dharma to make offerings to the Buddhas."

557a

Chapter XIV

Bestowal

1. At this point the Buddha told Maitreya Bodhisattva, "Maitreya, I now bestow on you this Dharma of *anuttarā samyaksaṃbodhi,* which I have accumulated over immeasurable *koṭi*s of *asaṃkhyeya*s of *kalpa*s. Sutras of this type should, during the final period after my nirvana, be circulated extensively throughout Jambudvīpa by you and others with your numinous power, so [the Dharma] is not cut off.

"Why? In the future time, there will be good men and women, as well as gods, dragons, demonic spirits, *gandharva*s, *rakṣasa*s, and so on, who will generate the intention to achieve *anuttarā samyaksaṃbodhi* and take pleasure in the great Dharma. If they are unable to hear sutras such as this, they will lose its good benefit. When people such as this hear these sutras, they must with great faith and joy realize their rarity and accept them with humility, explaining them extensively according to the benefits that sentient beings will receive from them.

2. "Maitreya, you should understand that bodhisattvas [may] have two [inferior] characteristics. What are these two? The first is the fondness for miscellaneous phrases and literary embellishment. The second is their lack of fear of penetrating deeply into the actualities of profound meanings.

"You should understand that it is novice bodhisattvas who are fond of miscellaneous phrases and literary embellishment. Those who lack the fear of entering into profound scriptures that are without defilement and without attachment, and who upon hearing them become pure in mind and accept and maintain, read and recite, and practice them as explained—you should understand that these [bodhisattvas] have been cultivating the path for a long time.

3. "Maitreya, there are two other *dharma*s (i.e., characteristics) regarding how those who are called novices are unable to be definite about the extremely profound Dharma. What are these two?

i) "The first is that when they hear profound sutras for the first time, they become fearful, generate doubts, and are unable to follow [those sutras]. Reviling them and lacking faith in them, they say 'I have not heard this before. Where did it come from?'

ii) "The second is that, when there are those who defend, maintain, and explain profound sutras such as these, [the novices] are unable to associate with [those teachers], make offerings to them, and revere them. Or, at times they talk about [the teachers'] transgressions and errors.

"You should understand that those who have these two *dharma*s are novice bodhisattvas. They only harm themselves, and they are unable to control their minds within the profound Dharma.

4. "Maitreya, there are two other *dharma*s concerning bodhisattvas who devoutly understand the profound Dharma, but who still harm themselves and are unable to attain forbearance of the nonarising of *dharma*s. What are these two?

i) "The first is to belittle novice bodhisattvas and not instruct them.

ii) "The second is to understand the profound Dharma, but with a discrimination that grasps at characteristics.

"These are the two *dharma*s."

5. When Maitreya heard this explanation he addressed the Buddha,

"World-honored One, this is unprecedented! It is as you have explained.

"I will distantly transcend such evils and maintain the Dharma of *anuttarā samyaksaṃbodhi* that the Tathāgata has accumulated over innumerable *asaṃkhyeya*s of *kalpa*s.

"If in the future there are good men and women who seek the Mahayana, I will make certain that they get hold of such sutras. Using their power of mindfulness, I will cause them to receive and maintain, read and recite, and extensively explain them for others.

"World-honored One, if in the latter age there are those able to receive, maintain, read, recite, and explain them for others, one should understand that these will all be established by Maitreya's numinous power."

The Buddha said, "Excellent, excellent, Maitreya! It is as you have explained. I am happy for you!"

6. At this all the bodhisattvas held their palms together and addressed the Buddha, "We too, after the Buddha's nirvana, will extensively disseminate the Dharma of *anuttarā samyaksaṃbodhi* throughout the countries of the ten directions. We will also guide those who explain the Dharma and cause them to obtain this sutra."

7. Then the four heavenly kings addressed the Buddha, "World-honored One, in every place, whether city, village, mountain forest, or wilderness, where there are those who read and recite and explain these fascicles of scripture, we will lead our palace retainers in proceeding to those places, to listen to the Dharma and protect those people. For an area of a hundred *yojana*s we will make it convenient [to hear their explanations] without seeking."

8. At this point the Buddha said to Ānanda, "Accept and maintain this sutra, and disseminate it extensively."

Ānanda said, "Assuredly. I have already accepted and maintained its essentials. World-honored One, what is the name of this sutra?"

The Buddha said,

"Ānanda, this sutra is named the 'Discourse of Vimalakīrti.' It is also called the 'Dharma Gate of the Inconceivable Emancipation.' As such you should accept and maintain it."

When the Buddha finished explaining this sutra, the Elder Vimalakīrti, Mañjuśrī, Śāriputra, Ānanda, and all the great congregations of gods, humans, and *asura*s, hearing what the Buddha had explained, rejoiced greatly.

End of Fascicle Three

Bibliography

Boin, Sara, trans. *The Teaching of Vimalakīrti (Vimalakīrtinirdeśa)*. London: Pali Text Society, 1976. English translation of Étienne Lamotte's French translation, listed below.

Lamotte, Étienne, trans. *L'enseignement de Vimalakīrti*. Louvain: Bibliothèque du Muséon, 1962.

Luk, Charles (Lu Ku'an Yü), trans. *The Vimalakīrti Nirdeśa Sūtra*. Berkeley, CA: Shambhala, 1972.

Nattier, Jan. *"The Teaching of Vimalakīrti [Vimalakīrtinirdeśa]*: A Review of Four English Translations," *Buddhist Literature* 2 (2000): 234–58.

Takasaki, Jikidō, and Kōshō Kawamura, trans. *"Yuima-gyō," Yuima-gyō, Shiyaku Bonten shomon kyō, Shuryōgon zammai kyō* [*Vimalakīrti Sūtra, Questions of the Brahmā (Deva) Viśeṣacinti Sūtra, and Śūraṃgamasamādhi Sūtra*], *Monju kyōten* [*Mañjuśrī Scriptures*] no. 2. Tokyo: Daizō shuppan, 1993.

Thurman, Robert A. F., trans. *The Holy Teaching of Vimalakīrti: A Mahāyāna Scripture*. University Park, PA and London: Pennsylvania University Press, 1976.

Watson, Burton, trans. *The Vimalakīrti Sutra*. New York: Columbia University Press, 1997.

Glossary

anuttarā samyaksaṃbodhi: Complete, perfect enlightenment. *See also bodhi.*

arhat ("one who is worthy" of offerings): A saint who has completely eradicated the passions and attained liberation from the cycle of birth and death (samsara); arhatship is the highest of the four stages of spiritual attainment in the Hinayana. *See also* Hinayana; samsara.

asura: A class of supernatural beings; a demigod.

bodhi: Enlightenment; the state of the highest perfection of wisdom; the state of undefiled purity and eternal bliss.

bodhicitta: Lit., "mind (*citta*) of enlightenment (*bodhi*)," the aspiration or intention to attain enlightenment undertaken by a bodhisattva in order to help other sentient beings to liberation. *See also* bodhisattva.

bodhisattva ("enlightenment being"): One who has engendered the profound aspiration to achieve enlightenment (*bodhicitta*) on behalf of all sentient beings, through the practice of the perfections (*pāramitā*s). The spiritual ideal of the Mahayana. *See also bodhicitta;* Mahayana; perfections.

bodhi tree: The tree under which a Buddha attains enlightenment.

Buddhahood: The state of becoming or being a Buddha; the goal of the bodhisattva path.

Buddha land: A cosmic world or realm in which a particular Buddha dwells. Also called Buddha country.

Buddha-nature: The potentiality of becoming a Buddha; the essential nature of a Buddha inherent in all sentient beings.

deva: A class of supernatural beings; a god or divine being.

dhāraṇī: Generally, a powerful verbal incantation or mantra; also, "to hold," as a container for good spiritual qualities. In earliest Mahayana texts the term refers to a mnemonic device for the recollection of Buddhist doctrine.

dharma: Any phenomenon, thing, or element; the elements that make up the perceived phenomenal world.

Dharma: The truth, law; the teachings of the Buddha.

Dharma body (*dharmakāya*): The manifestation of the Buddha as ultimate reality or suchness. *See also* suchness.

Dharma-nature: The essential nature of all that exists, same as true suchness and the Dharma body. *See also* Dharma body; suchness.

dhyāna: Meditation; a state of meditative concentration and absorption.

emptiness (*śūnyatā*): The absence of substantiality or inherent existence of the self and all phenomena (*dharmas*); all *dharmas* arise only through the dependent origination of causes and conditions (*pratītyasamutpāda*). Direct insight into emptiness is the attainment of *prajñā* (transcendental wisdom). *See also dharma; prajñā.*

enlightenment. *See bodhi.*

entrances (*āyatanas*): The six sense organs of eyes, ears, nose, tongue, body, and mind and their six corresponding objects—form, sound, smell, taste, tangible objects, and mental objects, totaling twelve. *See also* realms; sense organs; senses.

evil destiny or destination: Refers to rebirth in one of the three lower realms of samsaric existence, the realms of animals, hungry ghosts (*pretas*), or hell. *See also* samsara.

four continents: According to Buddhist cosmology, the four large land masses in the ocean around Mount Sumeru, each in one of the cardinal directions, which comprise the world of human beings. *See also* Mount Sumeru.

four correct postures: The four basic physical postures of walking, standing, sitting, and lying down; a Buddhist practitioner strives to maintain mindfulness in all of these postures. *See also* mindfulness.

four elements: The four physical elements that constitute material things (*dharmas*)—earth, fire, water, and wind.

four heavenly kings: The guardian gods of the four cardinal directions, rulers of the four continents. *See also* four continents.

four noble truths: The basic doctrine of Buddhism: 1) the truth of suffering, 2) the truth of the cause of suffering, 3) the truth of the cessation of suffering, and 4) the truth of the path that leads to nirvana. *See also* nirvana.

four unlimiteds (*brāhma-vihāras*): Four mental states or qualities to be cultivated by bodhisattvas—sympathy (*maitrī*), compassion (*karuṇā*), joy (*muditā*), and equanimity (*upekṣā*). Also called four unlimited states of mind.

gandharva: A heavenly musician.

garuḍa: A mythological being in the form of a giant bird.

Hinayana ("Small Vehicle"): A term applied by Mahayana Buddhists to various early schools of Buddhism whose primary soteriological aim is individual salvation. Hinayana followers are grouped into the two categories of *śrāvaka*s and *pratyekabuddha*s and there are four stages of spiritual attainment, culminating in arhatship. *See also* arhat; Mahayana; non-returner; once-returner; *pratyekabuddha; śrāvaka;* stream-enterer.

kalpa: An eon, an immensely long period of time.

kiṃnara: A class of mythological beings, half bird and half human, that make celestial music.

lion's roar: A metaphor for great eloquence in teaching the Dharma.

Mahayana: ("Great Vehicle"): A form of Buddhism that developed in India around 100 B.C.E. and which exalts as its religious ideal the bodhisattva, great beings who aspire to enlightenment on behalf of all sentient beings. *See also* bodhisattva.

mahoraga: A class of snake-like mythological beings.

Maitreya: The future Buddha, currently still a bodhisattva. *See also* bodhisattva.

Mañjuśrī: The bodhisattva who represents wisdom. *See also* bodhisattva.

Māra: The Evil One, the personification of the realm of desire; a symbol of the afflictions that hinder progress on the path to Buddhahood.

mindfulness: A fundamental Buddhist practice of maintaining awareness and clear observation during all one's activities, physical or mental, in order to bring the mind under control and to a state of rest and provide a stable basis for more profound knowledge and insight.

Mount Sumeru: In Buddhist cosmology, the highest mountain rising from the center of the world, surrounded by an ocean in which the four continents that comprise the world of human beings are situated. *See also* four continents.

nirvana: Liberation from samsara, a state in which all passions are extinguished and the highest wisdom attained; *bodhi,* enlightenment. *See also bodhi;* samsara.

non-returner (*anāgāmin*): The third of the four stages of spiritual attainment in the Hinayana; one who has attained this stage is no longer subject to rebirth in the realm of desire. *See also* Hinayana; triple world.

once-returner (*sakṛdāgāmin*): The second of the four stages of spiritual attainment in the Hinayana; one who has attained this state is subject to rebirth only once in each of the three realms of the triple world before attaining nirvana. *See also* Hinayana; nirvana; triple world.

One Vehicle (*ekayāna*): The Buddha vehicle, the Mahayana teaching that leads to complete enlightenment and attainment of Buddhahood, contrasted with the teachings of the two Hinayana vehicles. The One Vehicle includes and transcends all three vehicles of the *śrāvaka, pratyekabuddha,* and bodhisattva paths. *See also* vehicle.

pāramitā. See perfections.

perfections (*pāramitā*s): Six qualities to be perfected by bodhisattvas on their way to complete enlightenment—1) charity or giving (*dāna*), 2) discipline or morality (*śīla*), 3) forbearance or patience (*kṣānti*), 4) exertion or perseverance (*vīrya*), 5) meditation (*dhyāna*), and 6) wisdom (*prajñā*). *See also* bodhisattva.

prajñā: Transcendental, liberative wisdom; one of the perfections. *See also* perfections.

Prātimokṣa: A part of the Vinaya which contains the disciplinary rules for monastics. *See also* Vinaya.

pratyekabuddha ("solitary enlightened one"): One of the two kinds of Hinayana sages, along with *śrāvaka*s, who seek to reach the stage of arhat and attain nirvana. A *pratyekabuddha* attains liberation through direct observation and understanding of the principle of dependent origination without the guidance of a teacher, and does not teach others. *See also* arhat; Hinayana; nirvana; *śrāvaka.*

psychophysical elements, forces (*skandha*s): The five elements of form, feeling, conception, mental process, and consciousness which comprise the personality and give rise to the mistaken view of a permanent, inherent self.

rakṣasa: A type of demon.

realms (*dhātus*): The realms of sensory experience brought about by the interaction of the six sense organs with their corresponding objects, and their resulting consciousnesses, totaling eighteen. *See also* entrances; sense organs; senses.

Śākyamuni: The historical Buddha, who lived in India in the fifth century B.C.E. and whose life and teachings form the basis for Buddhism.

samādhi: A mental state of concentration, focusing the mind on one point; also a transcendent mental state attained by the repeated practice of concentration.

samsara: The cycle of existence, the continuous round of birth and death through which beings transmigrate; the world of suffering, contrasted with the bliss of nirvana. *See also* nirvana.

samyaksaṃbuddha: One who has attained complete, perfect enlightenment (*anuttarā samyaksaṃbodhi*).

Śāriputra: A principal disciple of the Buddha. In several Mahayana sutras such as the *Vimalakīrti Sutra* the figure of Śāriputra serves as an example of the inferior learning and understanding of the Hinayana *śrāvaka* path.

sense organs: The six sense organs of the eyes, ears, nose, tongue, body, and mind. *See also* entrances; realms; senses.

senses: The sense perceptions that correspond to the six sense organs—visual, auditory, olfactory, gustatory, tactile, and mental perceptions. *See also* entrances; realms; sense organs.

skillful means (*upāya*): The various methods and means used by Buddhas and bodhisattvas to guide and teach sentient beings, adapted to their different capacities.

śramaṇa: Mendicant, monk; another name for a Buddhist monk, originally applied to those who maintained an ascetic practice.

śrāvaka ("auditor"): Originally, a disciple of the Buddha, one of those who heard him expound the teachings directly; later, the term came to refer to one of the two kinds of Hinayana followers, along with *pratyekabuddhas*, to distinguish them from followers of the Mahayana. *See also* Hinayana; Mahayana; *pratyekabuddha*.

stream-enterer (*srota-āpanna*): The first of the four stages of spiritual attainment in the Hinayana; one who has entered the stream of the Dharma by destroying various wrong views. *See also* Hinayana.

suchness: Ultimate reality; the state of things as they really are. Insight into the suchness of all phenomena, i.e., as empty of inherent self-existence, arising only through dependent origination, is perfect wisdom (*prajñā*). *See* also emptiness; *prajñā*.

sutra: A Buddhist scripture, a discourse of the Buddha. Capitalized, the term refers to one of the three divisions of the Tripiṭaka. *See also* Tripiṭaka.

Tathāgata: An epithet for a Buddha, meaning one who has gone to (*gata*) and come from (*āgata*) suchness (*tathā*), i.e., the embodiment of the truth of suchness. *See also* suchness.

tathāgatagarbha: Lit., the "womb (*garbha*) of the Tathāgata," the inherent capacity for Buddhahood within all sentient beings. *See also* Buddhahood; Tathāgata.

Three Jewels: Buddha, Dharma (the teachings), and Sangha (the monastic community), also called the three refuges.

Tripiṭaka: The three divisions or "baskets" (*piṭaka*s) of the Buddhist canon: the Sutras, discourses and teachings of the Buddha; the Vinaya, codes of monastic discipline; and the Abhidharma, scholastic treatises on the Buddhist teachings.

triple world: The three realms of samsaric existence: the realm of desire (*kāmadhātu*), i.e., the world of ordinary consciousness accompanied by desires; the realm of form (*rūpadhātu*), in which desires have been eliminated but the physical body remains; and the formless realm (*ārūpya-dhātu*), in which the physical body no longer exists. *See also* samsara.

universal ruler (*cakravartin*): The ideal king, as conceived of in Indian philosophy. Also called wheel-turning sage king.

vehicle (*yāna*): The various Buddhist paths of practice. The Hinayana comprises the two vehicles of the *śrāvaka* and *pratyekabuddha,* contrasted with the bodhisattva vehicle of the Mahayana. *See also* Hinayana; Mahayana; One Vehicle; *pratyekabuddha; śrāvaka*.

Vinaya: Precepts and rules of conduct for monastics; along with the Abhidharma and the Sutras, one of the three divisions of the Tripiṭaka. *See also* Tripiṭaka.

yakṣa: A type of demon.

Index

A

Abhirati. *See* Wondrous Joy world
Accumulation of Eloquence 79
Accumulation of Fragrances
  167–71
Accumulation of Jewels 79
Accumulation of Wisdom 79
Achievement of All Benefits 146
act(s), action(s), activity(ies) (*see
  also* deed) 16, 25, 30, 31, 32–3,
  35, 43, 44, 52, 69, 163, 174, 178
  completion of 31, 35
  four all-embracing 15
  good 6, 26, 29, 163
  meritorious 6, 163
  pure 32–3, 80
  ten evil 151
  three types of 163
Adorned Purity 102, 103
affection 9, 112, 122, 127, 129, 141,
  150
affliction(s) 71, 77, 95, 98, 99, 111,
  113, 115, 118, 124, 127, 140, 142,
  144, 150, 151, 154, 177, 178, 180,
  181, 188
aggregation(s), empty 94, 98, 115
Ajita Keśakambala 99
Akaniṣṭha Heaven 188
Akṣobhya 68, 146, 185, 187, 188,
  189, 190
Amitābha 146
Amitāyurdhyāna-sūtra 69
Āmrapālī 77, 175

anāgāmin. See non-returner
Ānanda 58–9, 106, 107, 175, 176,
  177, 178, 179, 199
Anāthapiṇḍika's Park 11
anger 87, 99, 127, 139, 144, 149,
  150, 172
animals 15, 149, 156, 172
Aniruddha 102
anuttarā samyaksaṃbodhi (*see also*
  enlightenment, complete) 21,
  36, 70, 84, 94, 97, 98, 101, 103,
  104, 106, 109, 110, 113, 114, 116,
  118, 119, 127, 130, 136, 145, 148,
  151, 168, 174, 179, 180, 189, 190,
  192, 196, 197, 198, 199
arhat(s), arhatship (*see also* sage,
  sagely) 30, 31, 32, 33, 35, 44, 45,
  51, 52, 55, 139, 140, 148, 186
art(s) 25, 69, 155
aspiration 16, 19, 53, 58, 101, 160,
  180
assembly(ies) (*see also* congregation) 16, 57, 59, 68, 79, 88, 98,
  110, 115, 117, 119, 121, 152, 159,
  168, 169, 171, 175, 188
  charity 117, 118
  great 88, 130, 171
  of the three vehicles (*see also*
    sangha) 36, 37
asuras 59, 79, 134, 199
attachment(s) 92, 105, 110, 125,
  127, 129, 170, 186, 197
  defiled 132, 149

209

A List of the Volumes of
the BDK English Tripiṭaka
(First Series)

Abbreviations

Ch.:	Chinese
Skt.:	Sanskrit
Jp.:	Japanese
Eng.:	Published title
T.:	Taishō Tripiṭaka

Vol. No.		Title	T. No.
61-II	*Ch.* *Skt.*	Pien-chung-pien-lun （辯中邊論） Madhyāntavibhāga	1600
61-III	*Ch.* *Skt.*	Ta-ch'eng-ch'êng-yeh-lun （大乘成業論） Karmasiddhiprakaraṇa	1609
61-IV	*Ch.* *Skt.*	Yin-ming-ju-chêng-li-lun （因明入正理論） Nyāyapraveśa	1630
61-V	*Ch.* *Skt.*	Chin-kang-chên-lun （金剛針論） Vajrasūcī	1642
61-VI	*Ch.* *Eng.*	Chang-so-chih-lun （彰所知論） The Treatise on the Elucidation of the Knowable	1645
62	*Ch.* *Skt.*	Ta-ch'eng-chuang-yen-ching-lun（大乘莊嚴經論） Mahāyānasūtrālaṃkāra	1604
63-I	*Ch.* *Skt.*	Chiu-ching-i-ch'eng-pao-hsing-lun （究竟一乘寶性論） Ratnagotravibhāgamahāyānottaratantra-śāstra	1611
63-II	*Ch.* *Skt.*	P'u-t'i-hsing-ching （菩提行經） Bodhicaryāvatāra	1662
63-III	*Ch.*	Chin-kang-ting-yü-ch'ieh-chung-fa-a-nou-to- lo-san-miao-san-p'u-t'i-hsin-lun （金剛頂瑜伽中發阿耨多羅三藐三菩提心論）	1665
63-IV	*Ch.* *Skt.*	Ta-ch'eng-ch'i-hsin-lun （大乘起信論） Mahāyānaśraddhotpāda-śāstra (?)	1666
63-V	*Ch.* *Pāli*	Na-hsien-pi-ch'iu-ching （那先比丘經） Milindapañhā	1670
64	*Ch.* *Skt.*	Ta-ch'eng-chi-p'u-sa-hsüeh-lun（大乘集菩薩學論） Śikṣāsamuccaya	1636
65	*Ch.*	Shih-mo-ho-yen-lun （釋摩訶衍論）	1688
66-I	*Ch.* *Eng.*	Pan-jo-po-lo-mi-to-hsin-ching-yu-tsan （般若波羅蜜多心經幽賛） A Comprehensive Commentary on the Heart Sutra (Prajñāpāramitā-hṛdaya-sūtra)	1710

Vol. No.		Title	T. No.
66-II	*Ch.*	Kuan-wu-liang-shou-fo-ching-shu （觀無量壽佛經疏）	1753
66-III	*Ch.*	San-lun-hsüan-i （三論玄義）	1852
66-IV	*Ch.*	Chao-lun （肇論）	1858
67, 68	*Ch.*	Miao-fa-lien-hua-ching-hsüan-i （妙法蓮華經玄義）	1716
69	*Ch.*	Ta-ch'eng-hsüan-lun （大乘玄論）	1853
70-I	*Ch.*	Hua-yen-i-ch'eng-chiao-i-fên-ch'i-chang （華嚴一乘教義分齊章）	1866
70-II	*Ch.*	Yüan-jên-lun （原人論）	1886
70-III	*Ch.*	Hsiu-hsi-chih-kuan-tso-ch'an-fa-yao （修習止觀坐禪法要）	1915
70-IV	*Ch.*	T'ien-t'ai-ssŭ-chiao-i （天台四教儀）	1931
71, 72	*Ch.*	Mo-ho-chih-kuan （摩訶止觀）	1911
73-I	*Ch.*	Kuo-ch'ing-pai-lu （國清百錄）	1934
73-II	*Ch.* *Eng.*	Liu-tsu-ta-shih-fa-pao-t'an-ching （六祖大師法寶壇經） The Platform Sutra of the Sixth Patriarch	2008
73-III	*Ch.*	Huang-po-shan-tuan-chi-ch'an-shih-ch'uan- hsin-fa-yao （黃檗山斷際禪師傳心法要）	2012A
73-IV	*Ch.*	Yung-chia-chêng-tao-ko （永嘉證道歌）	2014
74-I	*Ch.* *Eng.*	Chên-chou-lin-chi-hui-chao-ch'an-shih-wu-lu （鎮州臨濟慧照禪師語錄） The Recorded Sayings of Linji (In Three Chan Classics)	1985
74-II	*Ch.* *Eng.*	Wu-mên-kuan （無門關） Wumen's Gate (In Three Chan Classics)	2005
74-III	*Ch.* *Eng.*	Hsin-hsin-ming （信心銘） The Faith-Mind Maxim (In Three Chan Classics)	2010

Vol. No.		Title	T. No.
74-IV	*Ch.*	Ch'ih-hsiu-pai-chang-ch'ing-kuei （勅修百丈清規）	2025
75	*Ch.*	Fo-kuo-yüan-wu-ch'an-shih-pi-yen-lu （佛果圜悟禪師碧巖録）	2003
	Eng.	The Blue Cliff Record	
76-I	*Ch.*	I-pu-tsung-lun-lun （異部宗輪論）	2031
	Skt.	Samayabhedoparacanacakra	
	Eng.	The Cycle of the Formation of the Schismatic Doctrines	
76-II	*Ch.*	A-yü-wang-ching （阿育王經）	2043
	Skt.	Aśokarāja-sūtra (?)	
	Eng.	The Biographical Scripture of King Aśoka	
76-III	*Ch.*	Ma-ming-p'u-sa-ch'uan （馬鳴菩薩傳）	2046
	Eng.	The Life of Aśvaghoṣa Bodhisattva (In Lives of Great Monks and Nuns)	
76-IV	*Ch.*	Lung-shu-p'u-sa-ch'uan （龍樹菩薩傳）	2047
	Eng.	The Life of Nāgārjuna Bodhisattva (In Lives of Great Monks and Nuns)	
76-V	*Ch.*	P'o-sou-p'an-tou-fa-shih-ch'uan （婆藪槃豆法師傳）	2049
	Eng.	Biography of Dharma Master Vasubandhu (In Lives of Great Monks and Nuns)	
76-VI	*Ch.*	Pi-ch'iu-ni-ch'uan （比丘尼傳）	2063
	Eng.	Biographies of Buddhist Nuns (In Lives of Great Monks and Nuns)	
76-VII	*Ch.*	Kao-sêng-fa-hsien-ch'uan （高僧法顯傳）	2085
	Eng.	The Journey of the Eminent Monk Faxian (In Lives of Great Monks and Nuns)	
76-VIII	*Ch.*	Yu-fang-chi-ch'ao: T'ang-ta-ho-shang-tung- chêng-ch'uan（遊方記抄: 唐大和上東征傳）	2089-(7)
77	*Ch.*	Ta-t'ang-ta-tz'ŭ-ên-ssŭ-san-ts'ang-fa-shih- ch'uan （大唐大慈恩寺三藏法師傳）	2053
	Eng.	A Biography of the Tripiṭaka Master of the Great Ci'en Monastery of the Great Tang Dynasty	

Vol. No.		Title	T. No.
78	*Ch.*	Kao-sêng-ch'uan （高僧傳）	2059
79	*Ch.*	Ta-t'ang-hsi-yü-chi （大唐西域記）	2087
	Eng.	The Great Tang Dynasty Record of the Western Regions	
80	*Ch.*	Hung-ming-chi （弘明集）	2102
81–92	*Ch.*	Fa-yüan-chu-lin （法苑珠林）	2122
93-I	*Ch.*	Nan-hai-chi-kuei-nei-fa-ch'uan （南海寄歸內法傳）	2125
	Eng.	Buddhist Monastic Traditions of Southern Asia	
93-II	*Ch.*	Fan-yü-tsa-ming （梵語雑名）	2135
94-I	*Jp.*	Shō-man-gyō-gi-sho （勝鬘經義疏）	2185
94-II	*Jp.*	Yui-ma-kyō-gi-sho （維摩經義疏）	2186
95	*Jp.*	Hok-ke-gi-sho （法華義疏）	2187
96-I	*Jp.*	Han-nya-shin-gyō-hi-ken （般若心經秘鍵）	2203
96-II	*Jp.*	Dai-jō-hos-sō-ken-jin-shō （大乘法相研神章）	2309
96-III	*Jp.*	Kan-jin-kaku-mu-shō （觀心覺夢鈔）	2312
97-I	*Jp.*	Ris-shū-kō-yō （律宗綱要）	2348
	Eng.	The Essentials of the Vinaya Tradition	
97-II	*Jp.*	Ten-dai-hok-ke-shū-gi-shū （天台法華宗義集）	2366
	Eng.	The Collected Teachings of the Tendai Lotus School	
97-III	*Jp.*	Ken-kai-ron （顯戒論）	2376
97-IV	*Jp.*	San-ge-gaku-shō-shiki （山家學生式）	2377
98-I	*Jp.*	Hi-zō-hō-yaku （秘藏寶鑰）	2426
	Eng.	The Precious Key to the Secret Treasury (In Shingon Texts)	
98-II	*Jp.*	Ben-ken-mitsu-ni-kyō-ron （辨顯密二教論）	2427
	Eng.	On the Differences between the Exoteric and Esoteric Teachings (In Shingon Texts)	

Vol. No.		Title	T. No.
104-V	*Jp.*	Kan-jin-hon-zon-shō （觀心本尊抄）	2692
	Eng.	Kanjinhonzonsho or The Most Venerable One Revealed by Introspecting Our Minds for the First Time at the Beginning of the Fifth of the Five Five Hundred-year Ages (In Two Nichiren Texts)	
104-VI	*Ch.*	Fu-mu-ên-chung-ching （父母恩重經）	2887
105-I	*Jp.*	Ken-jō-do-shin-jitsu-kyō-gyō-shō-mon-rui （顯淨土眞實教行証文類）	2646
	Eng.	Kyōgyōshinshō: On Teaching, Practice, Faith, and Enlightenment	
105-II	*Jp.*	Tan-ni-shō （歎異抄）	2661
	Eng.	Tannishō: Passages Deploring Deviations of Faith	
106-I	*Jp.*	Ren-nyo-shō-nin-o-fumi （蓮如上人御文）	2668
	Eng.	Rennyo Shōnin Ofumi: The Letters of Rennyo	
106-II	*Jp.*	Ō-jō-yō-shū （往生要集）	2682
107-I	*Jp.*	Has-shū-kō-yō （八宗綱要）	蔵外
	Eng.	The Essentials of the Eight Traditions	
107-II	*Jp.*	San-gō-shī-ki （三教指帰）	蔵外
107-III	*Jp.*	Map-pō-tō-myō-ki （末法燈明記）	蔵外
	Eng.	The Candle of the Latter Dharma	
107-IV	*Jp.*	Jū-shichi-jō-ken-pō （十七條憲法）	蔵外